DEMOCRACY

OPPOSING VIEWPOINTS®

Other Books of Related Interest

DEMOCRACY

OPPOSING VIEWPOINTS®

Mike Wilson, *Book Editor*

Bonnie Szumski, *Publisher*
Helen Cothran, *Managing Editor*

OPPOSING
VIEWPOINTS®
SERIES

GREENHAVEN PRESS
An imprint of Thomson Gale, a part of The Thomson Corporation

THOMSON
™
GALE

Detroit • New York • San Francisco • San Diego • New Haven, Conn.
Waterville, Maine • London • Munich

LIBRARY OF CONGRESS CATALOGING-IN-PUBLICATION DATA

Democracy / Mike Wilson, book editor.
p. cm. — (Opposing viewpoints series)
Includes bibliographical references and index.
ISBN 0-7377-3315-2 (lib. : alk. paper) — ISBN 0-7377-3316-0 (pbk. : alk. paper)
1. Democracy 2. Religion and politics. 3. Elections—United States. 4. Terrorism.
I. Wilson, Mike, 1954– . II. Opposing viewpoints series (Unnumbered)
JC423.D415 2006
321.8—dc22   2005052333

Printed in the United States of America

> "Congress shall make no law...abridging the freedom of speech, or of the press."

First Amendment to the U.S. Constitution

The basic foundation of our democracy is the First Amendment guarantee of freedom of expression. The Opposing Viewpoints Series is dedicated to the concept of this basic freedom and the idea that it is more important to practice it than to enshrine it.

Contents

Why Consider Opposing Viewpoints?

"The only way in which a human being can make some approach to knowing the whole of a subject is by hearing what can be said about it by persons of every variety of opinion and studying all modes in which it can be looked at by every character of mind. No wise man ever acquired his wisdom in any mode but this."

John Stuart Mill

In our media-intensive culture it is not difficult to find differing opinions. Thousands of newspapers and magazines and dozens of radio and television talk shows resound with differing points of view. The difficulty lies in deciding which opinion to agree with and which "experts" seem the most credible. The more inundated we become with differing opinions and claims, the more essential it is to hone critical reading and thinking skills to evaluate these ideas. Opposing Viewpoints books address this problem directly by presenting stimulating debates that can be used to enhance and teach these skills. The varied opinions contained in each book examine many different aspects of a single issue. While examining these conveniently edited opposing views, readers can develop critical thinking skills such as the ability to compare and contrast authors' credibility, facts, argumentation styles, use of persuasive techniques, and other stylistic tools. In short, the Opposing Viewpoints Series is an ideal way to attain the higher-level thinking and reading skills so essential in a culture of diverse and contradictory opinions.

In addition to providing a tool for critical thinking, Opposing Viewpoints books challenge readers to question their own strongly held opinions and assumptions. Most people form their opinions on the basis of upbringing, peer pressure, and personal, cultural, or professional bias. By reading carefully balanced opposing views, readers must directly confront new ideas as well as the opinions of those with whom they disagree. This is not to simplistically argue that everyone who reads opposing views will—or should—change his or her opinion. Instead, the series enhances readers' understanding of their own views by encouraging confrontation with opposing ideas. Careful examination of others' views can lead to the readers' understanding of the logical inconsistencies in their own opinions, perspective on why they hold an opinion, and the consideration of the possibility that their opinion requires further evaluation.

Evaluating Other Opinions

To ensure that this type of examination occurs, Opposing Viewpoints books present all types of opinions. Prominent spokespeople on different sides of each issue as well as well-known professionals from many disciplines challenge the reader. An additional goal of the series is to provide a forum for other, less known, or even unpopular viewpoints. The opinion of an ordinary person who has had to make the decision to cut off life support from a terminally ill relative, for example, may be just as valuable and provide just as much insight as a medical ethicist's professional opinion. The editors have two additional purposes in including these less known views. One, the editors encourage readers to respect others' opinions—even when not enhanced by professional credibility. It is only by reading or listening to and objectively evaluating others' ideas that one can determine whether they are worthy of consideration. Two, the inclusion of such viewpoints encourages the important critical thinking skill of objectively evaluating an author's credentials and bias. This evaluation will illuminate an author's reasons for taking a particular stance on an issue and will aid in readers' evaluation of the author's ideas.

It is our hope that these books will give readers a deeper understanding of the issues debated and an appreciation of the complexity of even seemingly simple issues when good and honest people disagree. This awareness is particularly important in a democratic society such as ours in which people enter into public debate to determine the common good. Those with whom one disagrees should not be regarded as enemies but rather as people whose views deserve careful examination and may shed light on one's own.

Thomas Jefferson once said that "difference of opinion leads to inquiry, and inquiry to truth." Jefferson, a broadly educated man, argued that "if a nation expects to be ignorant and free . . . it expects what never was and never will be." As individuals and as a nation, it is imperative that we consider the opinions of others and examine them with skill and discernment. The Opposing Viewpoints Series is intended to help readers achieve this goal.

David L. Bender and Bruno Leone,
Founders

Greenhaven Press anthologies primarily consist of previously published material taken from a variety of sources, including periodicals, books, scholarly journals, newspapers, government documents, and position papers from private and public organizations. These original sources are often edited for length and to ensure their accessibility for a young adult audience. The anthology editors also change the original titles of these works in order to clearly present the main thesis of each viewpoint and to explicitly indicate the opinion presented in the viewpoint. These alterations are made in consideration of both the reading and comprehension levels of a young adult audience. Every effort is made to ensure that Greenhaven Press accurately reflects the original intent of the authors included in this anthology.

Introduction

"The only moral foundation of government is the consent of the people."

—John Adams, 1776

"A common passion or interest will, in almost every case, be felt by a majority of the whole. . . . Hence it is that such democracies have ever been spectacles of turbulence and contention; have ever been found incompatible with personal security or the rights of property; and have in general been as short in their lives as they have been violent in their deaths.

—James Madison, 1787

Democracy is essentially a contract between those who are governed and those who govern. The health of such a political system depends upon the governors exercising their power responsibly, and the governed educating themselves about the important issues of the day and holding their leaders accountable. When one party breaks the contract—when, for example, government officials abuse their power, or the people fail to stay informed—democracies decline or collapse. Examining the health of democracies around the world involves looking at how well leaders and citizens are fulfilling their end of the bargain. The importance of both parties meeting their obligations has long been understood as the cornerstone of democracy.

The creation of democracy owes a debt to the theories of certain philosophers of the Enlightenment Era, such as Jean Jacques Rousseau, Thomas Hobbes, and John Locke, who theorized that people were by nature free but gave up some freedoms to government in exchange for security. English philosopher John Locke, who greatly influenced America's founders, wrote,

> The only way whereby anyone devests (*sic*) himself of his Natural Liberty, and puts on the bonds of Civil Society is by agreeing with other Men to joyn (*sic*) and unite into a Community

for their comfortable, safe, and peaceable living one amongst another. . . . When any number of Men have so consented to make one Community or Government, they are thereby presently incorporated, and make one Body Politick, wherein the Majority have a Right to act and conclude the rest.

Locke identified three types of rights—delegated rights ceded to the government; retained rights not ceded but which could be ceded; and inalienable rights, rights that cannot ever be ceded to the government. The founders drew on Locke's work when formulating these words in the Declaration of Independence: "All Men are created equal, that they are endowed by their Creator with certain unalienable Rights, that among those are Life, Liberty and the Pursuit of Happiness—That to secure these Rights, Governments are instituted among Men, deriving their just Powers from the Consent of the Governed."

Consent of the governed is the key to democracy's claim to legitimacy. James Wilson, one of the signers of the declaration, wrote, "The only reason why a free and independent man was bound by human laws was this—that he bound himself." The people of the United States consented to forming the federal government by adopting the Constitution, which defines government power and limits that power by identifying rights not ceded to government. Voters periodically consent to government by electing representatives to whom the power to govern is delegated. Consent can be withdrawn by voting against candidates. As Hans Morgantheau, author of the classic work *Politics Among Nations*, puts it, "What is the saving grace of democracy? . . . You can throw the scoundrels out!" The contract between a government and its people depends upon responsible leaders who act in the best interest of their constituencies. Built into all democracies is the means to oust such leaders when they fail to fulfill their side of the bargain. America's founders knew well that corrupt or incompetent leaders undermine democracy.

The founders also recognized that although bad leaders could harm a democracy, so too could citizens who fail to meet their obligations to stay informed and keep their representatives accountable. Founder James Madison pointed out that "a people who mean to be their own Governors, must arm themselves with the power which knowledge gives." According to Thomas Jefferson, "If a nation expects to be ignorant and free, in a state of civilization, it expects what never was and never will be." Jefferson believed that having an educated voting public was vital to the survival of democracy. He wrote that the "people themselves are [government's] only safe depositories. And to render them safe, their minds must be improved to a certain degree."

Informed consent also requires access to information about government. Senator John Cornyn of Texas observed in 2005 that "our founders . . . firmly believed that a free society couldn't exist without an informed citizenry and an open and accessible government." Jefferson said much the same thing more than two hundred years earlier: "Whenever the people are well-informed, they can be trusted with their own government; that, whenever things get so far wrong as to attract their notice, they may be relied on to set them right."

When citizens fail to educate themselves about the workings of their government and the major issues affecting their lives, disaster can strike. There have been cases where the populace has supported an incompetent or immoral leader. As Morgenthau notes, "If you define democracy as government with the consent of the people, then certain totalitarianisms have indeed been democracies. Take Nazism. If you define democracy in terms of government by the consent of the people, Hitler governed with the passionate and enthusiastic consent of the overwhelming majority of the people." The founders were aware of this risk, fearing a tyranny of the majority driven by passion or ignorance.

Gauging the health of democracies around the world requires an examination of how well the governors and the governed are upholding their end of the democratic bargain. The authors in *Opposing Viewpoints: Democracy* debate the state of this revered political system in the following chapters: What Is the State of Democracy? What Should Be the Relationship Between Religion and Democracy? Should U.S. Elections Be Reformed? Should Democracy Be Fostered Worldwide? The resources in this book provide readers with an opportunity to form their own opinions about the health, value, and future of democracy.

CHAPTER 1

What Is the State of Democracy?

Chapter Preface

When examining the state of democracy, many analysts compare how many democracies exist today compared to how many existed in the past. Such an analysis makes clear that the growth of democracy has come in waves. Political scientist Samuel Huntington's influential 1991 book, *The Third Wave: Democratization in the Late 20th Century*, describes this trend in the growth of democracy worldwide. Huntington defines governments as democratic "to the extent that [their] most powerful collective decisionmakers are selected through fair, honest and periodic elections in which candidates freely compete for votes and in which virtually all the adult population is eligible to vote." Using this definition, which scholars often call "electoral democracy," Huntington identifies three "waves" of democracy that have occurred over time.

The first wave Huntington identifies dates from 1828 to 1926. During this period, democracy spread within the United States. First, the right to vote was extended to most males, then to freed slaves, and then to women. Also during the same period, twenty-nine new democracies arose throughout the world. This first wave was followed by what Huntington calls a "reverse wave" from 1922 to 1942, as Italy, Germany, Spain, and Japan turned to fascism. By 1942 there were only twelve democracies in the world.

According to Huntington, the second wave of democracy occurred from 1943 to 1962. U.S. forces occupied parts of Europe and Japan after World War II, imposing or encouraging democratic institutions in those regions. Also, the breakup of the colonial empires of European powers after World War II led to the creation of new democracies around the world. By 1962 there were thirty-six democracies worldwide. However, the period after World War II also saw the spread of Communist ideology that competed with Western democracy for influence over other states. In some instances the United States helped overthrow democratically elected governments it feared would not favor U.S. interests. According to Huntington, a reversion to authoritarianism began, continuing through 1975.

Beginning in 1974, a third wave of democracy began, when military dictatorships were overthrown in Portugal and Greece. The military dictatorship in Spain was overthrown in 1976. Democracy spread to Latin America in the late 1970s and 1980s, and to sub-Saharan Africa in the 1990s. According to Larry Diamond, a senior research fellow at the Hoover Institution, 117 countries met Huntington's definition of democracy by 1996. The late 1990s saw a slowing of the third wave. Democratic reforms that had been implemented in several Arab countries during the 1980s were reversed. The rate of increase in electoral democracies decreased from 1991 until 1997, leading Diamond to speculate in 1999 that the third wave of democratization might be over.

Recent events make democracy enthusiasts hopeful, however. The United States invaded Afghanistan in 2001 and Iraq in 2003, and is working to help both nations democratize. Citizens in Georgia in 2003 and Ukraine in 2004 took to the streets to protest corrupt elections, and the leaders responsible no longer hold office. Syria had to withdraw from its occupation of Lebanon in 2005 after massive protests by the Lebanese. "Maybe, just maybe," political scientist Daniel W. Drezner observed in May 2005, "we're at the beginning of the fourth wave of democratization."

Whether or not a new wave of democracy is building remains the center of debate. Authors in this chapter examine the state of democracy today. The authors examine whether the spread of democracy has resulted in more freedom worldwide, whether democracy benefits all nations, and whether corporate power and global commerce help to spread or undermine democracy.

> "*Democracy has made more progress in the past quarter century than anyone could have imagined. Let that thought be our inspiration for the important tasks that lie ahead.*"

Democracy and Freedom Are Spreading Worldwide

David Lowe

In the following viewpoint David Lowe, vice president of Government and External Relations for the National Endowment for Democracy, describes the spread of democracy around the world, called by some the "Third Wave" of democracy, which began in the mid-1970s and continues to this day. Lowe defines democratic nations as countries where the principal positions of political power are filled through regular, free, fair, and competitive elections that reflect the will of the voters. He argues that democracies protect human rights most effectively and are best at improving the economic prospects of citizens.

As you read, consider the following questions:

1. Have many countries that were not democracies in 1974 are, as stated by Lowe, democracies today?
2. In the author's view, do most poor African countries prefer democracy or some other form of government?
3. What achievement does Indian Nobel Laureate Amartya Sen say was the most significant of the twentieth century?

David Lowe, "Expanding Democracy Around the World: Prospects and Challenges," Address to the Savannah Council on World Affairs, *National Endowment for Democracy*, September 18, 2003. Reproduced by permission.

Not only does history work in unpredictable ways, we are rarely able to see the path it is taking until well after the fact. By . . . 1980, the world was well into what the political scientist Samuel Huntington has termed the "Third Wave" of democracy, encompassing a period that began in the mid-1970s and whose end many commentators believe has not yet been reached. According to Prof. Huntington, this democratic wave began in Portugal, spread first across Southern Europe to Spain and Greece, shifted to Latin America before taking down the Berlin Wall and moving on to parts of Africa and Asia.

What has been its impact? Some numbers can help us appreciate the scope of the Third Wave of democracy (and I am grateful for Professor Larry Diamond, a pioneer in the area of democracy research, for these compilations): when it began in 1974, of the 150 existing countries, only 41 were democracies. Of the remaining 109, about half are democratic today. Of the 45 new states created since the Third Wave began, almost 3/4 are democracies. And there's more: the overwhelming number of states that became democratic during the Third Wave have remained so. Only 14 of the 125 democracies that have existed during the Third Wave have reverted to authoritarianism, and in nine of these, democracy has been subsequently restored. One more encouraging statistic: of the 36 countries that the United Nations Development Program classifies as having "low human development," nearly one of three is a democracy.

What Is Democracy?

Let me make it clear that by "democracy," I am referring to those countries where the principal positions of political power are filled through regular, free, fair, and competitive elections such that the will of the voters is reflected in the outcome and, if you don't like what they do in office, you can, as they say in Brooklyn and in parts of New Jersey, "throw the bums out."

Now, I realize that many of you might not find this so impressive. After all, isn't it possible to have free and fair elections simultaneously with violations of civil liberties, official corruption, and lack of protections for the rights of minorities? In fact, one could point to a number of countries where this is in fact the case.

So let us stipulate that free and fair elections (and keep in mind that I do NOT include as democracies those countries where dictators seek to legitimize themselves by conducting sham elections) are but a first step, albeit an important first step, toward achieving a system of government that protects minority rights, and promotes respect for the rule of law, free association, clean government, civilian control of the military, government accountability, etc. I call this "liberal" democracy, and it is the kind of political system that organizations such as mine [National Endowment for Democracy] both here and abroad are working toward helping to bring about.

But even if one is emphasizing the "liberal" part of democracy, the overall pattern is encouraging. In its annual survey of freedom in the world, the human rights organization Freedom House measures various aspects of freedom, both civil and political, classifying countries as "free," "not free," or "partly free." In 1973, not free countries outnumbered free countries by 69 to 43, roughly 3 to 2 (with 38 countries receiving the partly free designation). Today, the reverse is true, with free countries outnumbering not free countries 89 to 48, nearly 2-1, an all time high.

Having outlined for you the dramatic growth over the past quarter century or so, of both democracy and freedom around the world, I'd like in the time remaining to focus on two questions:

First, what are the prospects for the continued spread of democracy?

And second, why does it matter?

To gauge the prospects for the spread of democracy, we must first account for the success it has achieved over the past quarter of a century. . . .

Democracy Is a Universal Value

One interesting development during the third wave of democracy has been the number of poor countries, particularly in Africa and Asia, that have joined the club, including Benin, Mali, Malawi, Mozambique, Bangladesh and Nepal. And what makes this most impressive is that survey data is be-

Half of All Countries Are Free

Freedom in the World

Not Free
49 Countries
(26%)

Free 89
Countries
(46%)

Partly Free
54 Countries
(28%)

Freedom and World Population

2,387,300,000
in Not Free
Countries
(37%)

2,819,080,000
in Free
Countries
(44%)

1,189,000,000
in Partly Free
Countries
(19%)

Freedom House, www.freedomhouse.org, 2005.

ginning to confirm what many democracy advocates have argued for years, namely, that democracy is not simply a western value. For example, in a poll conducted in 12 mainly poor African countries in 2001, about 2 of 3 say that democracy is "always preferable" to authoritarian rule and the same number reject one-party rule. An even higher number, 80%, reject military or one-man rule. In Latin America, where electoral democracies have often been plagued by problems of governance, support for democracy is a bit more ambivalent. Still, nearly 3 in 5 believe that democracy is always preferable, and only 15 per cent prefer an authoritarian regime. In East Asia and the post-Communist countries of Eastern Europe, the numbers supporting democracy are even higher.

The overwhelming conclusion is that after all the many isms the world has experienced over the past century, democracy is the only legitimate political doctrine that remains, or, as [former British prime minister Winston] Churchill famously put it, the worst form of government except for all the others. Why else would dictators such as Robert Mugabe of Zimbabwe, Alexander Lukashenka of Belarus, or even Fidel Castro seek to cloak their authoritarian rule in democratic clothing by holding "elections"?

The Indian Nobel Laureate Amartya Sen, who first came to world attention with his study of the relationship between democracy and the absence of famine, argues that of all the achievements of the twentieth century, the rise of democracy is the most significant. This has resulted largely from an attitudinal shift that has made the choice of democracy the metaphoric equivalent of the "default" setting in a computer program. "In considering democracy for a country that does not have it and where many people may not yet have the opportunity to consider it for actual practice," Sen contends, "it is now presumed that the people involved would approve of it once it becomes a reality in their lives."

In his celebrated speech at London's Westminster Palace twenty-one years ago, President [Ronald] Reagan offered a simple but eloquent argument for democracy:

> It would be cultural condescension, or worse, to say that any people prefer dictatorship to democracy. Who would voluntarily choose not to have the right to vote, decide to purchase government propaganda handouts instead of independent newspapers, prefer government to worker-controlled unions, opt for land to be owned by the state instead of those who till it, want government repression of religious liberty, a single political party instead of a free choice, a rigid cultural orthodoxy instead of democratic tolerance and diversity?

Lest I be accused of painting too rosy a picture, let me point out that democracy, which we [in the United States] take so for granted, faces many obstacles, particularly in countries that lack democratic traditions. . . .

Democracy Gaps

There are vast areas of the world where freedom and self-government continue to be denied. This so-called "democracy gap" is particularly striking in the countries of the Arab world, not one of which can be considered democratic. Because all countries in this category have predominantly Muslim populations, there is a tendency to blame religion for the gap. But that would ignore the reality that many non-Arab countries with Muslim majorities are, in fact, electoral democracies. In a fascinating article in the current edition of the *Journal of Democracy*, two respected political scientists who have examined the 47 Muslim majority states in the world conclude that not only do many countries in that category meet the test of electoral democracy, a number of them are what they term "overachievers," i.e., states which have achieved democracy in spite of low per capita income levels. Among those included in this category are Senegal, Mali, Bangladesh, and Indonesia.

Nonetheless, when it comes to the Arab world, the opposite is the case, namely, that democracy is unexpectedly absent even in those countries with high levels of per capita income, a variable, as I have pointed out, that otherwise correlates strongly with democracy.

Let me read from the conclusion of the Arab Human Development Report issued last year [2002] by the United Nations Development Programme [UNDP]:

> There is a substantial lag between Arab countries and other regions in terms of participatory governance. The wave of democracy that transformed governance in the 1980s and 1990s has barely reached the Arab States. This freedom deficit undermines human development and is one of the most painful manifestations of lagging political development.

How do we account for the lack of democracy in Arab countries? Let's go back to the argument that economic development correlates with democratization. There is one exception to this rule, and that is in those countries where virtually all economic growth can be accounted for by a single commodity, usually oil. As Fareed Zakaria noted, in these countries, the easy income from oil has retarded the growth of an independent business sector while enabling authoritarian rulers both to buy off their populations without having to tax them and to invest heavily in state security structures that stifle political dissent. This pattern, while existing outside the Middle East, has been particularly characteristic of regimes we know all too well.

The Arab-Israeli conflict has also worked to the benefit of the region's authoritarian regimes, by providing them the opportunity to divert potential dissent against them by channeling it against others, such as the U.S., for its support of Israel. That is why the UNDP report is so significant. It was written entirely by Arab scholars, advised by policy makers throughout the region, exhibiting the quality of self-criticism that has been all too rare in that part of the world. In this vein let me recommend a web site, the invaluable Middle East Media Research Institute, which makes a point of highlighting liberal voices in the region, which are so frequently drowned out by state-controlled media.

Closing the Democracy Gap

Indeed, one should not think that movement toward democracy is impossible in Arab countries. There are, in fact, small but significant signs of progress in countries such as Yemen, where opposition groups freely criticize the president and elections held last April were praised by western monitors; and in Bahrain, where parliamentary elections were held last year for the first time in 30 years, where women participate both in voting and in standing for election, and which now allows genuinely independent trade unions.

And though there are many ways to look at what is happening today in Iraq that can justify both hope and deep concern, one thing is clear: tyrants in the region and elsewhere are looking at the situation there with great fear. As the Middle East scholar Bernard Lewis notes: "An open and democratic regime in Iraq, inevitably with a Shiite majority, could arouse new hopes among the oppressed peoples of the region, and offer a corresponding threat to their oppressors."

Of course, I do not want to leave the impression that a democracy deficit exists in only one part of the world. As we know, there is the problem of failed states, notably on the African continent, that breeds war and misery, not to mention terrorism. But even in Africa there are signs of progress and hope, from the breakthrough in South Africa, which will celebrate its first decade of freedom next year, to the mere recent one in Kenya, where just last year the political opposition was able to replace the long ruling dictator, Daniel Arap Moi, with a new leadership whose ambitious platform includes tackling corruption, economic and social issues, and political reform. . . .

Which brings us to the question of why it matters so much that this wave of democracy not be reversed or that democracy be allowed to spread to new countries. There are few postulates that are as accepted among students of international relations as the one holding that democracies do not fight one another, except through words and occasional trade rifts. (Some recent examples will remain unspoken.) For it remains true that democracies do not export terrorism, or proliferate weapons of mass destruction, both current major national security concerns. Nor do they create mass flows of refugees, a concern of many of our allies, including new and fragile democracies that could be easily destabilized under such circumstances. By and large, democracies make the best protectors of human rights. And although the relationship is not absolute, there is some very compelling evidence that democracies are far more reliable than other systems in improving the economic prospects of their citizens.

As former Secretary of State Madeleine Albright has observed:

> Dictators impose; democracy is chosen. Nor is democracy a religion, but it is a faith that has lifted the lives of people in every corner of the globe.

So let me close with the observation that while we fight the war on terrorism through the traditional instruments of the military and law enforcement, we should not ignore the impact of assisting those individuals, groups, and governments working to make the transition to democracy. Although the benefits are so self-evident to us, we need to be mindful of the fact that democracy is not an easy system to sustain, particularly for countries whose people lack those habits of the heart that are its natural foundation. And yet, democracy has made more progress in the past quarter century than anyone could have imagined. Let that thought be our inspiration for the important tasks that lie ahead.

"Close to half of the 'democratizing' countries in the world are illiberal democracies."

The Spread of Democracy Does Not Always Result in More Freedom

Fareed Zakaria

In the following viewpoint Fareed Zakaria, editor of *Newsweek International*, challenges the notion that democracy necessarily results in more freedom. He says that the spread of democracy worldwide has actually undermined liberty in some regions. Citing examples throughout the world, Zakaria claims that some democracies have elected authoritarian leaders who have instituted an "illiberal democracy" that undermines the rule of law. This selection is from Zakaria's best-selling book *The Future of Freedom: Illiberal Democracy at Home and Abroad*.

As you read, consider the following questions:
1. In the author's view, how many Latin American countries that have held elections still experience human rights abuses incompatible with liberal democracy?
2. How have multiparty elections in sub-Saharan Africa affected the stability and honesty of government there, in the opinion of the author?
3. What is the central conflict between constitutional liberalism and democracy, in the view of Zakaria?

In contrast to the Western and East Asian models, during the last two decades in Africa and in parts of Asia and Latin America, dictatorships with little background in constitutional liberalism or capitalism have moved toward democracy. The results are not encouraging. In the Western Hemisphere, with elections having been held in every country except Cuba, a 1993 study by one of the leading scholars of democratization, Stanford's Larry Diamond, determined that ten of the twenty-two principal Latin American countries had "levels of human rights abuse that are incompatible with the consolidation of [liberal] democracy." Since then, with a few important exceptions such as Brazil, things have only gotten worse.

Consider Venezuela's Hugo Chavez. A colonel in the army, he was cashiered and jailed for his part in an unsuccessful coup d'état in 1992. Six years later, running on an angry, populist platform, he was elected president with a solid 56 percent of the vote. He proposed a referendum that would replace Venezuela's constitution, eviscerate the powers of the legislature and the judiciary, and place governing authority under a "Constituent Assembly." The referendum passed with 92 percent of the vote. Three months later his party won 92 percent of the seats in the new assembly. The proposed new constitution increased the president's term by one year, allowed him to succeed himself, eliminated one chamber of the legislature, reduced civilian control of the military, expanded the government's role in the economy, and allowed the assembly to fire judges. "We are heading toward catastrophe," warned Jorge Olavarria, a longtime legislator and former Chavez supporter. "This constitution will set us back 100 years, and the military will become an armed wing of the political movement." The new constitution passed in December 1999 with 71 percent of the vote. Despite the fact that Venezuela went through grim economic times during his first few years, Chavez never dropped below 65 percent in public approval ratings.

By early 2002 it seemed as if his luck was finally running out. Public discontent with his thuggish rule and a failing economy combined to spark massive demonstrations. The army and business elites plotted a coup and, in March 2002,

Chavez was ousted—for two days. Chavez, who is skilled at organizing "people power"—and who was helped by the blatantly undemocratic nature of the coup—was comfortably back in power within a week.

Venezuela has the telltale sign of democratic dysfunction: abundant natural resources, including the largest oil reserves outside the Middle East. This has meant economic mismanagement, political corruption, and institutional decay. Four out of five Venezuelans live below the poverty line in a country that, twenty years ago, had among the highest living standards in Latin America. In some ways the country was ripe for a revolution. But what it got was a new caudillo, a strongman who claims to stand up for his country against the world (which usually means the United States). This is why Chavez has shown his admiration for Fidel Castro, Saddam Hussein, and even the loony Mu'ammar Gadhafi.[1] More dangerously, Chavez represents a persistent hope in Latin America that constructive change will come not through a pluralist political system, in which an array of political parties and interests grind away at the tedious work of incremental reform, but in the form of some new, messianic leader who can sweep away the debris of the past and start anew. This tendency has been gaining ground throughout the Andean region in the last few years. If Latin America's economic woes persist, it could become more widespread.

Illiberal Democracy in Africa and Central Asia

In Africa the past decade has been a crushing disappointment. Since 1990, forty-two of the forty-eight countries of sub-Saharan Africa have held multiparty elections, ushering in the hope that Africa might finally move beyond its reputation for rapacious despots and rampant corruption. The *New York Times* recently compared this wave of elections to the transitions in eastern Europe after the fall of communism. This is a highly misleading analogy, however. Although democracy has in many ways opened up African politics and brought people liberty, it has also produced a

1. Fidel Castro, president of Cuba, Saddam Hussein, former president of Iraq, and Mu'ammar Gadhafi, president of Libya; all are leaders with whom the United States has had poor relations in the past.

Russian Democracy Is Failing

The leaders of the West must recognize that our current strategy towards Russia is failing. Our policies have failed to contribute to the democratic Russia we wished for and the people of this great country deserve after all the suffering they have endured. It is time for us to rethink how and to what extent we engage with [Vladimir] Putin's Russia and to put ourselves unambiguously on the side of democratic forces in Russia. At this critical time in history when the West is pushing for democratic change around the world, including in the broader Middle East, it is imperative that we do not look the other way in assessing Moscow's behaviour or create a double standard for democracy in the countries which lie to Europe's East. We must speak the truth about what is happening in Russia. We owe it to . . . the tens of thousands of Russian democrats who are still fighting to preserve democracy and human freedom in their country.

"An Open Letter to the Heads of State and Government of the European Union and NATO," Project for New American Century, September 28, 2004. www.newamericancentury.org.

degree of chaos and instability that has actually made corruption and lawlessness worse in many countries. One of Africa's most careful observers, Michael Chege, surveyed the wave of democratization in the 1990s and concluded that the continent had "overemphasized multiparty elections . . . and correspondingly neglected the basic tenets of liberal governance." These tenets will prove hard to come by, since most of Africa has not developed economically or constitutionally. It is surely not an accident that the two countries in Africa that are furthest along on the path toward liberal democracy, South Africa and Botswana, have per capita incomes above the zone of transition to democracy, which was from $3,000 to $6,000. South Africa's is $8,500 and Bostwana's $6,600; both are artificially high because of natural-resource wealth. None of this is to say that Africa was better off under its plundering dictators, but it does suggest that what Africa needs more urgently than democracy is good governance. There are some extraordinary success stories, such as Mozambique, which ended a sixteen-year civil war and is now a functioning democracy with a market economy. But it has had enormous help in establishing good government from the international community and the United Nations, a pattern unlikely to recur in every African country.

In Central Asia, elections, even when reasonably free, as in Kyrgyzstan, have resulted in strong executives, weak legislatures and judiciaries, and few civil and economic liberties. Some countries have held no elections; there, popular autocrats hold sway. Azerbaijan's president, Gaidar Aliyev, for example, is a former head of the Soviet-era intelligence bureau, the KGB, and a former member of the Soviet Politburo. He ousted his predecessor in a coup in 1993, but most serious observers of the region suspect that if a free and fair election were held today, Aliyev would win. Even when heroes become leaders, it doesn't seem to change much. Georgia is run by the venerated Eduard Shevardnadze, [former Soviet leader Mikhail] Gorbachev's reformist foreign minister who helped end the Cold War. Still, Shevardnadze rigs elections in his favor (even though he would probably win a free one) and runs a country in which corruption, is pervasive and individual liberties insecure.

Trend to Democracy

Naturally, illiberal democracy runs along a spectrum, from modest offenders such as Argentina to near-tyrannies such as Kazakhstan, with countries such as Ukraine and Venezuela in between. Along much of the spectrum, elections are rarely as free and fair as in the West today, but they do reflect popular participation in politics and support for those elected. The mixture of democracy and authoritarianism varies from country to country—Russia actually holds freer elections than most—but all contain these seemingly disparate elements. The only data base that scores countries separately on their democratic and constitutional records shows a clear rise in illiberal democracy over the last decade. In 1990 only 22 percent of democratizing countries could have been so categorized; in 1992 that figure had risen to 35 percent; in 1997 it was 50 percent, from which peak it has since declined somewhat. Still, as of this writing close to half of the "democratizing" countries in the world are illiberal democracies.

Yet some call it simply a passing phase, the growing pains that young democracies must endure. The *Economist* has argued that constitutional liberalism "is more likely to occur in a democracy." But is this commonly asserted view true? Do elections in places such as Central Asia and Africa open up political space in a country, forcing broader political, economic, and legal reforms? Or do these elections provide a cover for authoritarianism and populism? It is too soon to tell—most of these transitions are still underway—but the signs are not encouraging. Many illiberal democracies—almost all in Central Asia, for example—have quickly and firmly turned into dictatorships. Elections in these countries merely legitimized power grabs. In others, such as many in Africa, rapid moves toward democracy have undermined state authority, producing regional and ethnic challenges to central rule. Still others, such as Venezuela and Peru, retain some level of genuine democracy with lots of illiberal practices. Finally, there are cases such as Croatia and Slovakia, where an illiberal democratic system is evolving in a more constitutional and reformist direction. In these cases, the democratic element was a crucial spur to reform because it did what democracy does better than any other form of government: it threw the bums out, providing for a peaceful transfer of power from the old guard to a new regime. Note, however, that Croatia and Slovakia are both European countries with relatively high per capita incomes: $6,698 and $9,624, respectively. In general, outside Europe, illiberal democracy has not proved to be an effective path to liberal democracy.

Pakistan

Consider Pakistan. In October 1999, the Western world was surprised when Pakistan's army chief, General Pervez Musharraf, overthrew the freely elected prime minister, Nawaz Sharif. The surprising fact was not the coup—it was Pakistan's fourth in as many decades—but its popularity. Most Pakistanis were happy to be rid of eleven years of sham democracy. During that period, Sharif and his predecessor, Benazir Bhutto, abused their office for personal gain, packed the courts with political cronies, fired local governments, allowed Islamic fundamentalists to enact draconian laws, and plundered the state coffers. The headline of an essay in one of Pakistan's leading newspapers in January 1998 described the state of the country: "Fascist Democracy: Grab Power, Gag Opposition." Western, particularly American, newspapers had a very different reaction. Almost all righteously condemned the coup. During the 2000 presidential campaign, George W. Bush confessed to not remembering the name of the new Pakistani leader, but said that he would "bring stability to the region." The *Washington Post* immediately denounced him for uttering such heresies about a dictator.

Two years later and with the transforming events [surrounding the September 11, 2001, terrorist attacks] on his side, Musharraf had pursued a path of radical political, social, educational, and economic reform that even his supporters would not have predicted. Few elected politicians in Pakistan supported his moves. Musharraf has been able to promote these policies precisely because he did not have to run for office and cater to the interests of feudal bosses, Islamic militants, and regional chieftains. There was no guarantee that a dictator would do what Musharraf did. But in Pakistan no elected politician would have acted as boldly, decisively, and effectively as he did. As of this writing, Musharraf seems somewhat more autocratic and somewhat less liberal than he seemed at first flush. Yet he remains determined to modernize and secularize his country, although he is facing opposition from many feudal and religious factions in Pakistani society. Reforming Pakistan—economically and politically—is a near-impossible task. But as with Russia, if genuine liberalization and even democracy come to Pakistan it will come not because of its history of illiberal democracy but because it stumbled on a liberal autocrat.

Democracy Is Not Liberalism

Current concerns about elected autocrats in Russia, Central Asia, and Latin America would not have surprised nineteenth-century liberals such as John Stuart Mill. Mill opened his classic *On Liberty* by noting that as countries became democratic, people tended to believe that "too much importance had been attached to the limitation of [governmental] power itself. That . . . was a response against rulers whose interests were opposed to those of the people." Once the people were themselves in charge, caution was unnecessary; "The nation did not need to be protected against its own will." As if confirming Mill's fears, Aleksandr Lukashenko, after being elected president of Belarus overwhelmingly in a free 1994 election, when asked about limiting his powers, said, "There will be no dictatorship. I am of the people, and I am going to be for the people."

The tension between constitutional liberalism and democracy centers on the scope of governmental authority. Constitutional liberalism is about the limitation of power; democracy is about its accumulation and use. For this reason, many eighteenth- and nineteenth-century liberals saw democracy as a force that could undermine liberty. The tendency for a democratic government to believe it has absolute sovereignty (that is, power) can result in the centralization of authority, often by extraconstitutional means and with grim results. What you end up with is little different from a dictatorship, albeit one that has greater legitimacy.

"Democracy is important to people in developing countries [because it] recognizes their dignity as human beings."

The Spread of Democracy Benefits Developing Nations

Carl Gershman

According to Carl Gershman, president of the National Endowment for Democracy, in the following viewpoint, developing countries desire democracy more deeply than is appreciated by the established democracies in the West. These nations understand how democracy can benefit them, Gershman contends. Gershman argues that democracy benefits developing countries by holding leaders accountable; promoting economic development; enabling people to more effectively deal with natural disasters; promoting health, education, and overall well-being of citizens; encouraging peace; fostering learning through public discussion; and providing enrichment and dignity to citizens' lives.

As you read, consider the following questions:
1. In the view of philosopher Amartya Sen, quoted by the author, how does a country become fit for democracy?
2. In the author's view, how does democracy and a free press correlate with the ability of a people to deal with disasters like famines?
3. Why does the author believe democracy promotes peace?

On the occasion of India's 50th anniversary in 1997, the New Delhi-based Centre for the Study of Developing Societies (CSDS) conducted a national survey assessing popular attitudes toward Indian democracy. The results constituted a stunning rejection of the common belief that the Indian people had lost faith in the country's democratic system. On the contrary, wrote Ashis Nandy, the director of the CSDS, "The democratic system enjoys greater legitimacy today than in the past. The poor and the deprived defend democracy more vigorously than the elite." Democracy's appeal, he said, owed a great deal to the Indians' belief that its inclusiveness offered the best way to deal with the country's staggering ethnic, religious, linguistic, and regional diversities. The poor especially valued democracy, according to Nandy, because they are convinced that "their votes matter," and they seem to relish exercising their franchise in defiance of their professional well-wishers among the more affluent classes who have their own ideas about what the poor need.

While the CSDS survey and Nandy's commentary focused only on India, they contained an important message about the importance of democracy to the peoples of other countries in the developing world. At the time the survey of Indian opinion appeared, Lee Kwan Yew and some other political leaders were advancing the argument that democracy was a Western system unsuited to Asian culture. This "Asian values" thesis was given a respectful hearing in elite circles in Asia and in *Foreign Affairs* and other Western publications. Its credibility was buttressed by the strength of East Asian economies that seemed to suggest that systems based on dominant parties, unaccountable elites, and large corporations favored by the state offered a rapid route to development for non-Western countries. This thesis quickly went out of fashion with the Asian financial crisis of 1997, the chief cause of which was the absence of democratic accountability and transparency in the principal institutions of government and finance. Suddenly, the views put forth by Nandy and other proponents of democracy in the developing world gained new force and a wider hearing. Democracy was seen to have as much relevance in Asian and other developing countries as in the West, not just as an effective system of governance but also as the way to achieve a better life for ordinary people.

The idea that ordinary people in developing countries benefit from democracy and, therefore, desire it and are willing to sacrifice to achieve it is still not widely understood or accepted in the established democracies of the West. Though we live in a period of globalization, most people in established democracies have little contact with the developing world. What they read about in the press or see on television are often disasters of one kind or another, leading to the view that many countries may not be "fit" for democracy. The economist and philosopher Amartya Sen has a ready answer for this view: "A country does not have to be deemed fit for democracy," he writes in an essay entitled "Democracy as a Universal Value" (*Journal of Democracy*, July 1999); "rather, it has to become fit through democracy."

Democracy Makes a Country "Fit"

How democracy can help a country become "fit" is a complex and subtle process that doesn't lend itself to news-bites. Let me suggest seven ways that democracy contributes to this process. The first is by offering the means by which the citizenry can hold governments accountable for their policies and integrity. The political scientist Larry Diamond has written that "predatory, corrupt, wasteful, abusive, tyrannical, incompetent governance is the bane of development." There is simply no way to control or eliminate corruption if people don't have access to the fundamental institutions of democracy: a free media that can expose corruption, an independent judiciary that can punish its perpetrators, and a system of free and fair elections that can hold political leaders accountable and, where appropriate, kick the rascals out. This doesn't mean that democracy will automatically reduce corruption or produce good governance. Responsible governance requires political will, effective institutions, professional officials, and an informed, alert, and aroused citizenry. But without democracy none of these things are possible, and the absence of political and legal restraints leads inevitably to abusive and corrupt behavior.

The second way is by promoting economic development

and prosperity. In the past, the conventional wisdom has held that development and prosperity encourage democracy, as better off citizens become more educated and have the ability to participate in politics and government. More recent analysis shows that the causal effect also works the other way around—democracy fosters development. This is a principal conclusion of the *Human Development Report 2002*, published by the United Nations Development Program, which notes that "democratic governance can trigger a virtuous cycle of development—as political freedom empowers people to press for policies that expand social and economic opportunities, and as open debates help communities shape their priorities."

The Spread of Democracy Benefits the World

The promotion of democracy globally benefits not only the citizens of recipient countries, but also helps other democratic nations and the international system as well. By expanding the global community of democracies and supporting emerging democracies in their development, the United States seeks to build a more secure and economically prosperous world in which individuals can live freely and enjoy healthy and productive lives.

Paula J. Dobriansky, "Shining a Light: U.S. Efforts to Strengthen Democracy Worldwide," August 2003. http://usinfo.state.gov.

In fact, research has shown that democracy not only helps people influence government policy but aids development in even more fundamental ways by fostering productive economic activity. Richard Roll and John R. Talbott, in a study published in the *Journal of Democracy* (July 2003), conclude that more than 80 percent of the cross-country variation in per capita income growth among developing countries (using data compiled for 1995–99) can be explained by factors that are aspects of democracy, among them the presence of strong property rights, political rights, civil liberties, and press freedom. They also found that dramatic increases in per capita income in developing countries have tended to follow democratic events (such as the removal of a dictator), and that antidemocratic events have tended to be followed by a reduction in economic growth.

The variables that contribute to economic growth share two characteristics. The first is that they represent institutions and policies that establish a rule of law enforced with fairness and justice. This encourages economic participants to work, take risks, save, and engage in other forms of productive economic activity. The second characteristic is that the variables constitute forms of collective action at the level of government—the enforcement of contracts, the protection of political and property rights, and the collection of taxes that can be used for public services. Such actions constitute important components of democratic governance, which explains why developing societies have so much to gain by establishing democratic systems.

Democracy and Disaster

The third way democracy helps the people in developing societies is by giving them the means to influence the actions of their respective governments in countering the effects of economic and social disasters. Here we are especially indebted to the work of Amartya Sen, who has shown that "in the terrible history of famines in the world, no substantial famine has ever occurred in any independent and democratic country with a relatively free press." The reason is that democracy, by empowering people at the grass roots, gives governments the political incentive to guard against famines or to take preventive measures to relieve human suffering if there is a danger of mass hunger. Precisely because famine or other kinds of disasters would be fatal to the citizens, not taking protective measures would be fatal to any government in a situation where the people are in a position to register their views. The protective power of democracy, Sen points out, might not be missed when things are going smoothly, but it becomes critically important to the most vulnerable parts of the population when a calamity looms that may arise from changed economic circumstances or accumulated policy mistakes.

The fourth way democracy helps developing societies become "fit" is by stimulating governments to promote the health, education, and overall well-being of their citizens. A study conducted by Patricio Navia and Thomas D. Zweifel (*Journal of Democracy*, July 2003) shows that since the end of the Cold War, the infant mortality rate in democracies (45.9 per 1,000 live births) is significantly lower than in non-democracies (50.5). Navia and Zweifel conclude that "at an equal level of development, on average five out of every one thousand newborns will die only and needlessly because the land of their birth is not democratically governed." Even benevolent dictatorships, they find, are always outperformed by democracies, for the simple reason that democratic governments are naturally more responsive than dictatorships to the needs of the people and are thus prepared to invest in social services to improve the citizens' quality of life.

Democracy and Peace

The fifth way democracy enriches the life of people in developing societies is by promoting peace, both between states and within them. The idea that democracy is a pacifying force owes a great deal to the work of R.J. Rummel, whose multi-volume work, *Understanding Conflict and War* (published between 1975–81), concluded that "Violence does not occur between free societies." [Philosopher] Immanuel Kant had reached the same conclusion nearly two centuries earlier in his essay "Perpetual Peace," where he noted that if "the consent of the citizenry is required in order to determine whether or not there will be war, it is natural that they consider all its calamities before committing themselves to so risky a game." Greater sensitivity to the cost of war is just one of the reasons that democracy fosters peace. James Lee Ray, in an essay entitled "The Democratic Path to Peace" (*Journal of Democracy*, April 1997), has also emphasized democracy's capacity to moderate the day-to-day relations among states, thereby preventing crises from developing to the point where they have to be peacefully resolved. We have also seen from the Indian case that democracy is an inclusive system that offers a way of accommodating ethnic and religious differences that are a principal source of conflict in the contemporary world.

The sixth way democracy helps people in developing societies is by making it possible for them to learn from one another through public discussion, thereby facilitating the definition of needs, priorities, and duties. Sen calls this the constructive role of democracy since it involves the formation of values and the generation of "informed and considered choices." Through public discussion, he notes, the people of the Indian states of Kerala and Tamil Nadu have come to understand and internalize the harmful effects of high fertility rates on the community and on the lives of young women. The result is that Kerala now has a fertility rate similar to that of Britain and France and lower than China's, a result achieved without coercion. Having people take ownership of an approach to solving a social problem through the formation of new values is ultimately far more effective than having a solution imposed or mandated by the government or by international assistance agencies. But such constructive action can't happen without democracy.

The seventh and final reason democracy is important to people in developing countries is that it enriches their lives as citizens and recognizes their dignity as human beings. Sen calls this the intrinsic value of democracy. People value political participation in the life of the community for its own sake, not because it advances a practical purpose. To be denied such participation, Sen writes, is "a major deprivation" since "exercising political rights is a crucial part of good lives of individuals as social beings." As we have seen, freedom serves many purposes since it makes it possible for people to defend their interests, expand their potential, and create new opportunities for themselves, their families, and their communities. This is what is meant by "the pursuit of happiness." But human freedom does not require an instrumental justification. It is important in itself.

Devotion to Democracy

Throughout the developing world there are people and organizations that are prepared to make great sacrifices in the pursuit of democracy, human rights, and political freedom. The courage and perseverance of democracy activists in Africa, woman's rights activists in the Middle East, and human rights defenders in Burma and other Asian autocracies refutes the notion that democracy is a Western system without appeal to people in the developing world. In fact, the very opposite is true. Not only is democracy needed and desired by people in developing countries, but their devotion to democracy often puts to shame citizens of the established democracies, who too often take democracy for granted and have become somewhat jaded in their appreciation of democracy's benefits to their own lives. It is not surprising that democracy's most impassioned advocates today should come from countries where democracy is least secure. Perhaps this will remind those who are fortunate enough to live in secure democracies to value what they have—and also to help those living where freedom is less secure to fulfill their aspirations for a democratic future.

"*The global spread of markets and democracy is a principal, aggravating cause of group hatred and ethnic violence throughout the non-Western world.*"

The Spread of Democracy Causes Ethnic Strife in Developing Nations

Amy Chua

In the following viewpoint, taken from her book *World on Fire: How Exporting Free Market Democracy Breeds Ethnic Hatred and Global Instability*, Amy Chua contends that democracy does not always benefit developing nations as its advocates claim. She argues that it can cause ethnic strife and can even result in "ethnic cleansing," where one ethnic group attempts to destroy or oust another. Democracy allows impoverished ethnic majorities to elect demagogues that scapegoat minorities that hold—or held—political and economic power, she claims. Chua is a professor at Yale Law School. She delivers lectures on globalization to government, business, and academic groups around the world.

As you read, consider the following questions:
1. How has the global spread of free markets and democracy affected the world's opinion of America, in Chua's opinion?
2. According to the author, how did ethnic backlash manifest itself in Zimbabwe?
3. What genocides does the author claim that the democracy backlash helped cause?

[There is] a phenomenon—pervasive outside the West yet rarely acknowledged, indeed often viewed as taboo —that turns free market democracy into an engine of ethnic conflagration. The phenomenon I refer to is that of *market-dominant minorities:* ethnic minorities who, for widely varying reasons, tend under market conditions to dominate economically, often to a startling extent, the "indigenous" majorities around them.

Market-dominant minorities can be found in every corner of the world. The Chinese are a market-dominant minority not just in the Philippines but throughout Southeast Asia. In 1998, Chinese Indonesians, only 3 percent of the population, controlled roughly 70 percent of Indonesia's private economy, including all of the country's largest conglomerates. More recently, in Burma, entrepreneurial Chinese have literally taken over the economies of Mandalay and Rangoon. Whites are a market-dominant minority in South Africa—and, in a more complicated sense, in Brazil, Ecuador, Guatemala, and much of Latin America. Lebanese are a market-dominant minority in West Africa. Ibo are a market-dominant minority in Nigeria. Croats were a market-dominant minority in the former Yugoslavia. And Jews are almost certainly a market-dominant minority in post-Communist Russia.

Market-dominant minorities are the Achilles' heel of free market democracy. In societies with a market-dominant ethnic minority, markets and democracy favor not just different people, or different classes, but different ethnic groups. Markets concentrate wealth, often spectacular wealth, in the hands of the market-dominant minority, while democracy increases the political power of the impoverished majority. In these circumstances the pursuit of free market democracy becomes an engine of potentially catastrophic ethnonationalism, pitting a frustrated "indigenous" majority, easily aroused by opportunistic vote-seeking politicians, against a resented, wealthy ethnic minority. This confrontation is playing out in country after country today, from Indonesia to Sierra Leone, from Zimbabwe to Venezuela, from Russia to the Middle East.

Since [the terrorist attacks of] September 11, 2001, this confrontation has also been playing out in the United States.

Americans are not an ethnic minority (although we are a national-origin minority, a close cousin). Nor is there democracy at the global level. Nevertheless, Americans today are everywhere perceived as the world's market-dominant minority, wielding outrageously disproportionate economic power relative to our size and numbers. As a result, we have become the object of mass, popular resentment and hatred of the same kind that is directed at so many other market-dominant minorities around the world.

Global anti-Americanism has many causes. One of them, ironically, is the global spread of free markets and democracy. Throughout the world, global markets are bitterly perceived as reinforcing American wealth and dominance. At the same time, global populist and democratic movements give strength, legitimacy, and voice to the impoverished, frustrated, excluded masses of the world—precisely the people, in other words, most susceptible to anti-American demagoguery. In more non-Western countries than Americans would care to admit, free and fair elections would bring to power anti-market, anti-American leaders. For the last twenty years Americans have been grandly promoting both marketization and democratization throughout the world. In the process we have directed at ourselves the anger of the damned.

The Panacea of Free Market Democracy

The relationship between free market democracy and ethnic violence around the world is inextricably bound up with globalization. But the phenomenon of market-dominant minorities introduces complications that have escaped the view of both globalization's enthusiasts and its critics.

To a great extent, globalization consists of, and is fueled by, the unprecedented worldwide spread of markets and democracy. For over two decades now, the American government, along with American consultants, business interests, and foundations, has been vigorously promoting free market democracy throughout the developing and post-socialist worlds. At times our efforts have bordered on the absurd. There is, for example, the sad tale of a delegation of American free market advisers in Mongolia. Just before they leave the country, the Americans are thrilled when a Mongolian official asks them to send more copies of the voluminous U.S. securities laws, photocopied on one side of the page. Alas, it turned out that the Mongolian was interested in the documents not for their content, but for the blank side of each page, which would help alleviate the government's chronic paper shortage.

There was also the time that the U.S. government hired New York–based Burson-Marsteller, the world's largest public relations firm, to help sell free market capitalism to the people of Kazakhstan. Among other ideas, Burson-Marsteller developed a television soap opera mini-series glorifying privatization. In one episode, two hapless families desperately want a new house but don't know how to build it. Suddenly a hot-air balloon descends from the sky, bearing the name "Soros Foundation" in huge letters. Americans spring out, erect the house, and soar away, leaving the awe-struck Kazakhstanis cheering wildly.

In the end, however, stories about American naïveté and incompetence are just a sideshow. The fact is that in the last two decades, the American-led global spread of markets and democracy has radically transformed the world. Both directly and through powerful international institutions like the World Bank, International Monetary Fund, and World Trade Organization (WTO), the United States government has helped bring capitalism and democratic elections to literally billions of people. At the same time, American multinationals, foundations, and nongovernmental organizations (NGOs) have swept the world, bringing with them ballot boxes and Burger Kings, hip-hop and Hollywood, banking codes and American-drafted constitutions.

The prevailing view among globalization's supporters is that markets and democracy are a kind of universal prescription for the multiple ills of underdevelopment. Market capitalism is the most efficient economic system the world has ever known. Democracy is the fairest political system the world has ever known and the one most respectful of individual liberty. Working hand in hand, markets and democracy will gradually transform the world into a community of prosperous, war-shunning nations, and individuals into liberal, civic-minded citizens and consumers. In the process,

Russian Democracy Has Resulted in Ethnic Strife

Russia—and most of Soviet society—was woefully unprepared for the democratic changes that were slowly imposed from the top. . . .

As a result, the government swiftly began to lose its authority in large parts of the country, ceding its former powers to the rapidly-developing local authorities that sought to "even the score" for past decades of abuse by the Communist state. The result was the rise of ethnic strife in the Caucasus, Central Asia and the Baltics. While many of the grievances on behalf of some local populations were legitimate, the Soviet government, fearing a general countrywide uprising against its rule, responded with force. That further galvanized local forces bent on maintaining their policies, resulting in massive outbreaks of ethnic conflict in the Caucasus and in other parts of the country.

Yevnegy Bedersky, *Power and Interest News Report*, February 23, 2005. www.pinr.com.

---

ethnic hatred, religious zealotry, and other "backward" aspects of underdevelopment will be swept away.

Thomas Friedman has been a brilliant proponent of this dominant view. In his best-selling book *The Lexus and the Olive Tree*, he reproduced a Merrill Lynch ad that said "The spread of free markets and democracy around the world is permitting more people everywhere to turn their aspirations into achievements," erasing "not just geographical borders but also human ones." Globalization, Friedman elaborated, "tends to turn all friends and enemies into 'competitors.'" Friedman also proposed his "Golden Arches Theory of Conflict Prevention" which claims that "no two countries that both have McDonald's have ever fought a war against each other. . . ." (Unfortunately, notes Yale history professor John Gaddis, "the United States and its NATO [North Atlantic Treaty Organization] allies chose just that inauspicious moment to begin bombing Belgrade, where there was an embarrassing number of golden arches.")[1]

---

1. NATO and U.S. forces began bombing targets in Yugoslavia on March 24, 1999, following breakdowns in peace negotiations to end ethnic strife and warfare in Yugoslavia.

For globalization's enthusiasts, the cure for group hatred and ethnic violence around the world is straightforward: more markets and more democracy. Thus after the September 11 attacks, Friedman published an op-ed piece pointing to India and Bangladesh as good "role models" for the Middle East and arguing that the solution to terrorism and militant Islam is: "Hello? Hello? There's a message here. It's democracy, stupid!"—"[m]ulti-ethnic, pluralistic, free-market democracy."

Ethnic Anti-Market Backlash

[To the contrary], the global spread of markets and democracy is a principal, aggravating cause of group hatred and ethnic violence throughout the non-Western world. In the numerous societies around the world that have a market-dominant minority, markets and democracy are not mutually reinforcing. Because markets and democracy benefit different ethnic groups in such societies, the pursuit of free market democracy produces highly unstable and combustible conditions. Markets concentrate enormous wealth in the hands of an "outsider" minority, fomenting ethnic envy and hatred among often chronically poor majorities. In absolute terms the majority may or may not be better off—a dispute that much of the globalization debate fixates on—but any sense of improvement is overwhelmed by their continuing poverty and the hated minority's extraordinary economic success. More humiliating still, market-dominant minorities, along with their foreign-investor partners, invariably come to control the crown jewels of the economy, often symbolic of the nation's patrimony and identity—oil in Russia and Venezuela, diamonds in South Africa, silver and tin in Bolivia, jade, teak, and rubies in Burma.

Introducing democracy in these circumstances does not transform voters into open-minded cocitizens in a national community. Rather, the competition for votes fosters the emergence of demagogues who scapegoat the resented minority and foment active ethnonationalist movements demanding that the country's wealth and identity be reclaimed by the "true owners of the nation." As America celebrated the global spread of democracy in the 1990s, ethnicized political slogans proliferated: "Georgia for the Georgians," "Eritreans

Out of Ethiopia," "Kenya for Kenyans," "Venezuela for *Pardos*," "Kazakhstan for Kazakhs," "Serbia for Serbs," "Croatia for Croats," "Hutu Power," "Assam for Assamese," "Jews Out of Russia." Romania's 2001 presidential candidate Vadim Tudor was not quite so pithy. "I'm Vlad the Impaler," he campaigned; referring to the historically economically dominant Hungarian minority, he promised: "We will hang them directly by their Hungarian tongue!"

When free market democracy is pursued in the presence of a market-dominant minority, the almost invariable result is backlash. This backlash typically takes one of three forms. The first is a backlash against markets, targeting the market-dominant minority's wealth. The second is a backlash against democracy by forces favorable to the market-dominant minority. The third is violence, sometimes genocidal, directed against the market-dominant minority itself.

Zimbabwe today is a vivid illustration of the first kind of backlash—an ethnically targeted anti-market backlash. For several years now President Robert Mugabe has encouraged the violent seizure of 10 million acres of white-owned commercial farmland. As one Zimbabwean explained, "The land belongs to us. The foreigners should not own land here. There is no black Zimbabwean who owns land in England. Why should any European own land here?" Mugabe himself was more explicit: "Strike fear in the heart of the white man, our real enemy!" Most of the country's white "foreigners" are third-generation Zimbabweans. Just 1 percent of the population, they have for generations controlled 70 percent of the country's best land, largely in the form of highly productive three-thousand-acre tobacco and sugar farms.

Watching Zimbabwe's economy take a free fall as a result of the mass landgrab, the United States and United Kingdom together with dozens of human rights groups urged President Mugabe to step down, calling resoundingly for "free and fair elections." But the idea that *democracy* is the answer to Zimbabwe's problems is breathtakingly naive. Perhaps Mugabe would have lost the 2002 elections in the absence of foul play. Even if so, it is important to remember that Mugabe himself is a product of democracy. The hero of Zimbabwe's black liberation movement and a master manipulator of masses, he swept to victory in the closely monitored elections of 1980, promising to expropriate "stolen" white land. Repeating that promise has helped him win every election since. Moreover, Mugabe's land-seizure campaign was another product of the democratic process. It was deftly timed in anticipation of the 2000 and 2002 elections, and deliberately calculated to mobilize popular support for Mugabe's teetering regime.

Ethnic Cleansing

In the contest between an economically powerful ethnic minority and a numerically powerful impoverished majority, the majority does not always prevail. Instead of a backlash against the market, another likely outcome is a backlash against democracy, favoring the market-dominant minority at the expense of majority will. Examples of this dynamic are extremely common. Indeed, . . . the world's most notorious cases of "crony capitalism" all involve a market-dominant ethnic minority—from Ferdinand Marcos's Chinese-protective dictatorship in the Philippines to President Siaka Stevens's shadow alliance with five Lebanese diamond dealers in Sierra Leone to President Daniel Arap Moi's "business arrangements" with a handful of Indian tycoons in Kenya today.

The third and most ferocious kind of backlash is majority-supported violence aimed at eliminating a market-dominant minority. Two recent examples are the ethnic cleansing of Croats in the former Yugoslavia and the mass slaughter of Tutsi in Rwanda. In both cases a resented and disproportionately prosperous ethnic minority was attacked by members of a relatively impoverished majority, incited by an ethnonationalist government. In other words, markets and democracy were among the causes of both the Rwandan and Yugoslavian genocides.

"Corporations . . . are structured to make money. In the pursuit of this one goal, they will freely cast aside concerns about the societies and ecological systems in which they operate."

Corporations Threaten Democracy

Lee Drutman and Charlie Cray

In this viewpoint Lee Drutman and Charlie Cray argue that corporations have corrupted democratic institutions. Corporations have undermined democracy, claim the authors, by pouring millions of dollars into conservative think tanks and policy organizations established to shape public opinion and governmental policymaking to advance the corporate agenda at the expense of the public interest. Drutman and Cray also argue that citizens are being manipulated by corporations to care more about their next purchases than about the state of their government. Lee Drutman is the communications director of Citizen Works and Charlie Cray is the director of the Center for Corporate Policy.

As you read, consider the following questions:

1. Of the one hundred largest economies in the world, how many of them are corporations, according to the authors?
2. Who outlined a plan for corporate leaders to target campuses, the courts, and the media as key battlegrounds for enhancing corporate power, according to the authors?

At a time when our democracy appears to be so thoroughly under the sway of large corporations, it is tempting to give up on politics. We must resist this temptation. Democracy offers the best solution to challenging corporate power. We must engage as citizens, not just as consumers or investors angling for a share of President [George W.] Bush's "ownership society."

Unfortunately, the destructive power of large corporations today is not limited to the political sphere. The increasing domination of corporations over virtually every dimension of our lives—economic, political, cultural, even spiritual—poses a fundamental threat to the well-being of our society.

Corporations have fostered a polarization of wealth that has undermined our faith in a shared sense of prosperity. A corporate-driven consumer culture has led millions of Americans into personal debt, and alienated millions more by convincing them that the only path to happiness is through the purchase and consumption of ever-increasing quantities of material goods. The damage to the earth's life-supporting systems caused by the accelerating extraction of natural resources and the continued production, use, and disposal of life-threatening chemicals and greenhouse gases is huge and, in some respects, irreversible.

Today's giant corporations spend billions of dollars a year to project a positive, friendly and caring image, promoting themselves as "responsible citizens" and "good neighbors." They have huge marketing budgets and public relations experts skilled at neutralizing their critics and diverting attention from any controversy. By 2004, corporate advertising expenditures were expected to top $250 billion, enough to bring the average American more than 2,000 commercial messages a day.

The problem of the corporation is at root one of design. Corporations are not structured to be benevolent institutions; they are structured to make money. In the pursuit of this one goal, they will freely cast aside concerns about the societies and ecological systems in which they operate.

When corporations reach the size that they have reached today, they begin to overwhelm the political institutions that can keep them in check, eroding key limitations on their destructive capacities. Internationally, of the 100 largest economies in the world, 51 are corporations and 49 are nations.

How Business Became So Powerful

Corporations in the United States began as quasi-government institutions, business organizations created by deliberate acts of state governments for distinct public purposes such as building canals or turnpikes. These corporations were limited in size and had only those rights and privileges directly written into their charters. As corporations grew bigger and more independent, their legal status changed them from creatures of the state to independent entities, from mere business organizations to "persons" with constitutional rights.

The last three decades have represented the most sustained pro-business period in U.S. history.

The corporate sector's game plan for fortifying its power in America was outlined in a memo written in August 1971 by soon-to-be Supreme Court Justice Lewis F. Powell Jr. at the behest of the U.S. Chamber of Commerce. The "Powell Memorandum," drafted in response to rising popular skepticism about the role of big business and the unprecedented growth of consumer and environmental protection laws, was intended as a catalytic plan to spur big business into action. Powell argued that corporate leaders should single out the campuses, the courts and the media as key battlegrounds.

One of the most significant developments that followed Powell's memo was the formation of the Business Roundtable in 1972 by Frederick Borch of General Electric and John Harper of Alcoa. As author Ted Nace has explained, "The Business Roundtable . . . functioned as a sort of senate for the corporate elite, allowing big business as a whole to set priorities and deploy its resources in a more effective way than ever before. . . . The '70s saw the creation of institutions to support the corporate agenda, including foundations, think tanks, litigation centers, publications, and increasingly sophisticated public relations and lobbying agencies."

For example, beer magnate Joseph Coors, moved by Powell's memo, donated a quarter of a million dollars to the

Analysis and Research Association, the forerunner of the massive font of pro-business and conservative propaganda known today as the Heritage Foundation. Meanwhile, existing but tiny conservative think tanks, like the Hoover Institute and the American Enterprise Institute for Public Policy Research, grew dramatically in the '70s. Today, they are key players in the pro-business policy apparatus that dominates state and federal policymaking.

According to a 2004 study by the National Committee for Responsive Philanthropy, between 1999 and 2001, 79 conservative foundations made more than $252 million in grants to 350 "arch-conservative policy nonprofit organizations." By contrast, the few timid foundations that have funded liberal causes often seem to act as a "drag anchor" on the progressive movement, moving from issue to issue like trust fund children with a serious case of attention-deficit disorder.

The Need to Act

The vast majority of people, when asked, believe that corporations have too much power and are too focused on making a profit. "Business has gained too much power over too many aspects of American life," agreed 82 percent of respondents in a June 2000 *Business Week* poll, a year and a half before Enron's collapse. A 2004 Harris poll found that three-quarters of respondents said that the image of large corporations was either "not good" or "terrible."

Corporations have achieved their dominant role in society through a complex power grab that spans the economic, political, legal and cultural spheres. Any attempt to challenge their power must take all these areas into account.

There is a great need to develop a domestic strategy for challenging corporate power in the United States, where 185 of the world's 500 largest corporations are headquartered. Although any efforts to challenge corporations are inevitably bound up in the global justice movement, there is much to do here in the United States that can have a profoundly important effect on the global situation.

By understanding the origin of the corporation as a creature of the state, we can better understand how we, as citizens with sovereignty over our government, ultimately can and must assert our right to hold corporations accountable. The task is to understand how we can begin to reestablish true citizen sovereignty in a country where corporations currently have almost all the power.

Developing the Movement

To free our economy, culture and politics from the grip of giant corporations, we will have to develop a large, diverse and well-organized movement. But at what level should we focus our efforts: local, state, national or global? The answer, we believe, is a balance of all four.

Across the country, many local communities continue to organize in resistance to giant chain stores like Wal-Mart, predatory lenders, factory farms, private prisons, incinerators and landfills, the planting of genetically modified organisms, and nuclear power plants. Local communities are continuously organizing to strengthen local businesses, raise the living wage, resist predatory marketing in schools, cut off corporate welfare and protect essential services such as water from privatization. Local struggles are crucial for recruiting citizens to the broader struggle against corporate rule.

Unfortunately, examples of grassroots movements that have succeeded in placing structural restraints on corporations are not as common as they should be. One of the ways we can accelerate the process is by organizing a large-scale national network of state and local lawmakers who are interested in enacting policies that address specific issues or place broader restraints on corporate power.

Just as the corporations have the powerful American Legislative Exchange Council (ALEC) to distribute and support model legislation in the states, so we need our own networks to experiment with and advance different policies that can curb and limit corporate power. The National Caucus of Environmental Legislators—a low-budget coalition of state lawmakers established in 1996 in response to the Republican takeover of Congress and several state legislatures—is a model that could be used to introduce and advance innovative legislative ideas at the state level. The New Rules Project has also begun to analyze and compile information on these kinds of laws. Additionally, the U.S. PIRG network of state public interest research groups and the Center for Policy Alternatives have worked to promote model progressive legislation, as has the newly founded American Legislative Issue Campaign Exchange (ALICE).

Wealth Will Control

We are creeping toward an oligarchic society where a relative handful of the rich and privileged decide, with their [corporate wealth], who will run, who will win, and how they will govern. I see no way to stop this trend without ending the arms race and establishing a system of campaign financing that reflects the values of fairness, political equality, and government accountability—the soul of democracy.

It won't be easy. The defenders of the present system will fight hard to hold on to their privilege, and they write the rules. Nothing short of an aroused public will change the system. Nothing less than democracy is at stake.

Bill Moyers, *Moyers on America: A Journalist and His Times*, 2004.

Despite their many strengths, many major movements of the past few decades (labor, environmental, consumer) have all suffered from internal fractures and a lack of connection to the broader society. The result is that they have been increasingly boxed into "special interest" roles, despite the fact that the policies they advocate generally benefit the vast majority of people.

Cognitive linguist George Lakoff puts it this way: "Coalitions with different interest-based messages for different voting blocks [are] without a general moral vision. Movements, on the other hand, are based on shared values, values that define who we are. They have a better chance of being broad-based and lasting. In short, progressives need to be thinking in terms of a broad-based progressive-values movement, not in terms of issue coalitions."

The Role of Labor

If there is one group at the center of the struggle to challenge corporate power, it is organized labor. As a Century Foundation Task Force Report on the Future of Unions concluded, "Labor unions have been the single most important agent for social justice in the United States."

Labor is at the forefront of efforts to challenge excessive CEO pay, corporate attempts to move their headquarters offshore to avoid paying their fair share of taxes, and the outsourcing of jobs. Labor also has played a leading role in opposing the war in Iraq and exposing war profiteers benefiting from Iraq reconstruction contracts.

As AFL-CIO President John Sweeney has written, unions need to start "building social movements that reach beyond the workplace into the entire community and offer working people beyond our ranks the opportunity to improve their lives and livelihood." This is beginning to occur more frequently. Union locals and national labor support groups like Jobs With Justice have been a key force in building crosstown alliances around economic justice battles such as living wage campaigns and the new Fair Taxes for All campaign.

These union-led, cross-community alliances have in turn supported some of the strongest union organizing campaigns, including the nearly two-decades-old Justice for Janitors campaign that the Service Employees International Union (SEIU) and its allies successfully organized in Los Angeles and other cities across the country.

Clearly, labor unions, along with community-based organizations and churches, will be central to the construction of lasting local coalitions that can serve as organizing clearinghouses to challenge corporate rule. . . .

Hyper-Commercialization

In our hyper-commercialized culture, we spend far more time and energy thinking about what products we want to buy next instead of thinking about how we can change our local communities for the better, or affect the latest debates in Washington, D.C. or the state capitol. And when so much energy is spent on commercial and material pursuits instead of on collective and political pursuits, we begin to think of ourselves as consumers, not citizens, with little understanding of how or why we are so disempowered.

The restoration of democracy requires us to address the backstory behind this process of psychological colonization. It requires us to address the public policies and judicial doctrines that treat advertising as a public good—a tax-deductible business expense and a form of speech protected by the First Amendment. It's been so long since we have seriously addressed such fundamental questions that, as a result, the average American is now exposed to more than 100 commercial messages per waking hour. As of October 2003, there were 46,438 shopping malls in the United States, covering 5.8 billion square feet of space, or about 20.2 square feet for every man, woman and child in the United States. As economist Juliet Schor reports, "Americans spend three to four times as many hours a year shopping as their counterparts in Western European countries. Once a purely utilitarian chore, shopping has been elevated to the status of a national passion."

A consequence of the hyper-commercialization of our culture is that instead of organizing collectively, we often buy into the market-based ideology of individual choice and responsibility and assume that we can change the world by changing our personal habits of consumption. The politics of recycling offers a minor but telling example of how corporations manage to escape blame by utilizing the politics of personal responsibility. Although recycling is a decent habit, the message conveyed is that the onus for environmental sustainability largely rests upon the individual, and that the solutions to pollution are not to be found further upstream in the industrial system.

The personal choices we make are important. But we shouldn't assume that's the best we can do. We need to understand that it can't truly be a matter of choice until we get some more say in what our choices are. True power still resides in the ability to write, enforce and judge the laws of the land, no matter what the corporations and their personal-choice, market-centered view of the world instruct us to believe.

Rebuilding the Public Sphere

With increased corporate encroachment upon our schools and universities, our arts institutions, our houses of worship and even our elections, we are losing the independent institutions that once nurtured and developed the values and beliefs necessary to challenge the corporate worldview. These and other institutions and public assets should be considered valuable parts of a public "commons" of our collective heritage and therefore off limits to for-profit corporations.

"The idea of the commons helps us identify and describe the common values that lie beyond the marketplace," writes author David Bollier. "We can begin to develop a more textured appreciation for the importance of civic commitment, democratic norms, social equity, cultural and aesthetic concerns, and ecological needs. . . . A language of the commons also serves to restore humanistic, democratic concerns to their proper place in public policy-making. It insists that citizenship trumps ownership, that the democratic tradition be given an equal or superior footing vis-à-vis the economic categories of the market."

Changing the Rules

Much citizen organizing today focuses on influencing administrative, legislative and judicial processes that are set up to favor large corporations from the very start. Put simply, many of the rules are not fair, and until we can begin to collectively challenge this fundamental unfairness, we will continue to fight with one hand tied behind our backs. Instead of providing opportunities for people to organize collectively to demand real political solutions and start asking tough questions about how harmful policies become law in the first place, many community-based organizations seem content to merely clean up the mess left behind by failed economic policies and declining social services.

The most successful organizing happens when it is focused on specific demands. Two crucial reforms have great potential to aid the movement's ability to grow: fundamental campaign finance reform and media reform. Together, these could serve as a compelling foundation for a mass movement that challenges corporate power more broadly.

The movement for citizen-controlled elections, organized at the local level with support from national groups such as the Center for Voting and Democracy and Public Campaign, provides a useful framework for action for the broad spectrum of people who currently feel shut out of politics.

Media reform is also essential. With growing government secrecy and a corporate-dominated two-party political system, the role of independent media is more critical than ever. As [commentator] Bill Moyers suggested in his keynote address at the National Conference on Media Reform in 2003, "If free and independent journalism committed to telling the truth without fear or favor is suffocated, the oxygen goes out of democracy."

The media have always been and will continue to be the most important tool for communicating ideas and educating the public about ongoing problems. [Writer] Thomas Paine wrote more than 200 years ago:

> There is nothing that obtains so general an influence over the manners and morals of a people as the press; from *that* as from a fountain the streams of vice or virtue are poured forth over a nation.

History is replete with examples that show how critical the media's role has been in addressing the injustices of our society. For instance, many Progressive Era reforms came only in response to the investigative exposés of corporate abuses by muckraking journalists like Upton Sinclair and Ida Tarbell writing in popular magazines like *Collier's* and *Mc-Clure's*, these writers provided a powerful public challenge to the corruption of the Gilded Age.

Because of increased corporate consolidation of the media, coverage of all levels of government has been greatly reduced. When people are kept ignorant of what is happening in their communities, in their states, in Washington, D.C. and in the world, it becomes much easier for large corporations to overwhelm the political process and control the economy without citizens understanding what is happening. Though media reform is a complex subject, one approach bears mentioning—establishing and strengthening non-profit media outlets.

Though campaign finance reform and media reform offer useful starting points, ultimately, there is much more to be done. We need to get tough on corporate crime. We need to make sure markets are properly competitive by breaking up the giant corporate monopolies and oligarchies. We need to make corporations more accountable to all stakeholders and less focused on maximizing shareholder profit above all. We need to stop allowing corporations to claim Bill of Rights protections to undermine citizen-enacted laws.

Ultimately, we need to restore the understanding that in a democracy the rights of citizens to govern themselves are more important than the rights of corporations to make money. Since their charters and licenses are granted by citizen governments, it should be up to the people to decide how corporations can serve the public good and what should be done when they don't. As Justices Byron White, William Brennan and Thurgood Marshall noted in 1978: "Corporations are artificial entities created by law for the purpose of furthering certain economic goals. . . . The State need not permit its own creation to consume it."

Corporations Should Not Control

The many constituencies concerned with the consequences of corporate power are indeed a diverse group, and although this diversity can be a source of strength, it also makes it difficult to clearly articulate a vision for the struggle. What principles, then, can unite us?

One abiding faith that almost all of us share is that of citizen democracy: that citizens should be able to decide how they wish to live through democratic processes and that big corporations should not be able to tell citizens how to live their lives and run their communities. The most effective way to control corporations will be to restore citizen democracy and to reclaim the once widely accepted principle that corporations are but creatures of the state, chartered under the premise that they will serve the public good, and entitled to only those rights and privileges granted by citizen-controlled governments. Only by doing so will we be able to create the just and sustainable economy that we seek, an economy driven by the values of human life and community and democracy instead of the current suicide economy driven only by the relentless pursuit of financial profit at any cost.

Therefore, we must work assiduously to challenge the dominant role of the corporation in our lives and in our politics. We must reestablish citizen sovereignty, and we must restore the corporations to their proper role as the servants of the people, not our masters. This is the people's business.

"Governments that grant their citizens a large measure of freedom to engage in international commerce find it dauntingly difficult to simultaneously deprive them of political and civil liberties."

Corporations Can Foster Democracy

Daniel T. Griswold

In this viewpoint Daniel T. Griswold argues that there is a statistical correlation between economic openness and civil freedom, demonstrating that governments that grant economic freedom find it difficult to deprive their citizens of political and civil liberties. Promotion of international trade will therefore foster democracy in countries that participate, he contends. Griswold is director of the Cato Institute's Center for Trade Policy Studies. He has authored or co-authored studies on, among other subjects, globalization, the World Trade Organization, trade and manufacturing, immigration, and trade and democracy.

As you read, consider the following questions:

1. According to Griswold, what was happening when the first wave of democratization took place during the nineteenth century?
2. According to the author, the most economically open countries are how many times more likely to enjoy full political and civil freedoms as those that are economically closed?
3. In the author's view, what effect do tariffs and other barriers to international commerce have on civil liberties?

The reality of the world today broadly reflects those theoretical links between trade, free markets, and political and civil freedom. As trade and globalization have spread to more and more countries in the last 30 years, so too have democracy and political and civil freedoms. In particular, people who live in countries that are relatively open to trade are much more likely to live in democracies and enjoy full civil and political freedoms than those who live in countries relatively closed to trade. Nations that have followed a path of trade reform in recent decades by progressively opening themselves to the global economy are significantly more likely to have expanded their citizens' political and civil freedoms.

Twin Trends of Global Freedom

The recent trend toward globalization has been accompanied by a trend toward greater political and civil liberty around the world. In the past 30 years, cross-border flows of trade, investment, and currency have increased dramatically, and far faster than output itself. Trade barriers have fallen unilaterally and through multilateral and regional trade agreements in Latin America; the former Soviet bloc nations; East Asia, including China; and more developed nations as well.

During that same period, political and civil liberties have been spreading around the world. Thirty years ago democracies were the exception in Latin America, while today they are the rule. Many former communist states from the old Soviet Union and its empire have successfully transformed themselves into functioning democracies that protect basic civil and political freedoms. In East Asia, democracy and respect for human rights have replaced authoritarian rule in South Korea. Taiwan, Thailand, the Philippines, and Indonesia.

According to Freedom House, a New York–based human rights organization, the share of the world's population that enjoys full civil and political liberties has risen sharply in the past three decades. The share of the world's people who live in countries Freedom House classifies as "Free"—meaning "countries in which there is broad scope for open political competition, a climate of respect for civil liberties, significant independent civic life, and independent media"—has jumped from 35 percent in 1973 to 44 percent today. Meanwhile, the share of people living in countries classified as "Not Free"—"where basic political rights are absent and basic civil liberties were widely and systematically denied"—has dropped from 47 to 35 percent. The share of people living in countries classified as "Partly Free"—those "in which there is limited respect for political rights and civil liberties"—has increased slightly from 18 to 21 percent (see Figure 1).

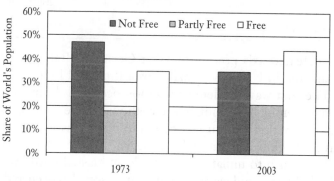

Figure 1. Expansion of Political and Civil Freedom, 1973 to 2003

Freedom House.

As globalization accelerated in the late 1980s after the fall of the Berlin Wall, so too did the global trend toward democracy. Again, according to Freedom House, the share of the world's governments that are democratically elected has spiked from 40 percent in the mid-1980s to 63 percent in 2002–03 (see Figure 2).

The world has experienced other periods of broad advancement in human liberty. Political scientist Samuel P. Huntington calls the most recent advance the "third wave of democratization." The first wave began early in the 19th century with the end of the Napoleonic Wars in Europe, when representative government took root in the United States; Great Britain; Switzerland; France; Britain's overseas dominions such as Canada, Australia, and New Zealand; and several smaller European states. The second wave began in the aftermath of World War II with the democratization of

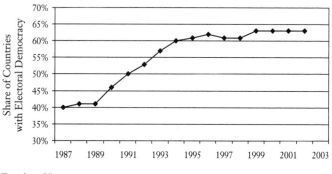

Figure 2. The Advance of Electoral Democracy, 1987 to 2002

Freedom House.

the defeated axis powers of West Germany, Italy, Austria, Japan, and in Uruguay, Brazil, Costa Rica, and India.

The first wave of democratization occurred during a period of rapidly expanding international trade and investment, a period known to economic historians as the first wave of globalization, which began in the 1840s with Britain's turn to unilateral free trade and lasted until World War I. The second wave of democratization also occurred in a time of expanding global trade as the more advanced economies turned away from the protectionism of the 1930s and embraced more open trade unilaterally and through successive rounds of negotiation in the General Agreement on Tariffs and Trade. In contrast, those periods that saw retreat from democracy (what Huntington calls "reverse waves") were also marked by broad retreats from free trade. In the first reverse wave, the 1920s and 1930s, the industrial countries increasingly turned to protectionism and economic nationalism; in the second reverse wave, in the 1960s and early 1970s, less developed countries turned inward as they embraced import substitution policies and hostility to foreign investment.

Critics who blame globalization for much of what is wrong in the world today cannot ignore the fact that globalization has been accompanied, in recent decades as well as in previous episodes of history, by the overwhelmingly positive phenomenon of more political and civil freedom for hundreds of millions of people around the world. Critics can dismiss the reality of those two powerful trends as a mere coincidence, but at the very least those trends undercut the argument that globalization has somehow been bad for democracy. During the most recent era of globalization, democracy and respect for individual political and civil freedoms have spread to a larger share of the human race than ever before.

Trade Correlates with Freedom

Behind the aggregate trends toward freedom is the question of whether those countries that have opened themselves to trade correlate with those that enjoy political and civil liberties today.

To measure the correlation between openness to trade and civil and political freedom among individual countries, this study uses two comprehensive and newly updated databases to compare economic and political/civil freedom in the world among a broad cross-section of countries. To measure political and civil freedom, we use Freedom House's annual *Freedom in the World* ratings. Freedom House rates virtually all of the world's nations and territories according to their political rights and civil liberties. The organization defines political rights as the ability of a nation's citizens "to participate freely in the political process. This includes the right to vote and compete for public office and to elect representatives who have a decisive vote on public policies." Civil liberties, according to the organization, "include the freedom to develop opinions, institutions, and personal autonomy without interference from the state."

To measure economic freedom and, more specifically, freedom to engage in international commerce, we use the Fraser Institute study, *Economic Freedom of the World*, which measures economic freedom in 123 countries. The study's authors, James Gwartney and Robert Lawson, measure economic freedom in five general areas: size of government; legal structure and security of property rights; access to sound money; regulation of credit, labor, and business; and freedom to exchange with foreigners. The last category will be used in this study to measure a nation's openness to trade and other forms of international commerce. The category includes taxes on international trade and nontariff regulatory trade barriers, the size of the trade sector, official versus blackmarket exchange rates, and restrictions on capital markets. Those countries rated by both databases encompass more than 90 percent of the world's population.

Comparing the two indexes reveals that nations with open and free economies are far more likely to enjoy full political and civil liberties than those with closed and state-dominated economies. The connection becomes evident when countries are grouped by quintiles according to their economic openness. Of the 25 rated countries in the top quintile of economic openness, 21 are rated "Free" by Freedom House and only one is rated "Not Free." In contrast, among the quintile of countries that are the least open economically, only seven are rated "Free" and nine are rated "Not Free". In other words, the most economically open countries are three times more likely to enjoy full political and civil freedoms as those that are economically closed. Those that are closed are nine times more likely to completely suppress civil

Figure 3. Economic Openness and Political/ Civil Freedom

Freedom House and *Economic Freedom of the World*.

and political freedoms as those that are open.

The percentage of countries rated as "Free" rises in each quintile as the freedom to exchange with foreigners rises, while the percentage rated as "Not Free" falls. In fact, 16 of the 19 countries rated as "Not Free" are found in the bottom two quintiles of economic openness, and only three in the top three quintiles. The percentage of nations rated as "Partly Free" also drops precipitously in the top two quintiles of economic openness (see Figure 4).

Figure 4. Political/Civil Freedom and Economic Openness

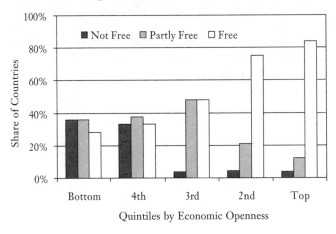

Freedom House and *Economic Freedom of the World.*

A more formal statistical comparison shows a significant, positive correlation between economic freedom, including the freedom to engage in international commerce, and political and civil freedom. The statistical correlation remains strong even when controlling for a nation's per capita gross domestic product, consistent with the theory that economic openness reinforces political liberty directly and independently of its effect on growth and income levels.

Specifically, a 1.0-point improvement in the 0-to-10 index measuring the freedom to exchange with foreigners implies, on average, a 0.6-point improvement in a comparable 0–10 combined index measuring political and civil freedom. That means that a country that rates a 9.0 on the scale of economic openness will on average rate 3.0 points higher on a comparable index of political and civil freedom compared to a country with the same per capita GDP but with a rating of 4.0 on the scale of economic openness. The same statistically significant correlation holds for a more general measure of economic freedom. Consistent with theory, economic freedoms, including freedom to exchange with foreigners, do in fact strongly correlate with political and civil freedoms.

One unmistakable lesson from the cross-country data is that governments that grant their citizens a large measure of freedom to engage in international commerce find it dauntingly difficult to simultaneously deprive them of political and civil liberties. A corollary lesson is that governments that "protect" their citizens behind tariff walls and other barriers to international commerce find it much easier to deny those same liberties.

Periodical Bibliography

The following articles have been selected to supplement the diverse views presented in this chapter.

Amnesty International   "People's Republic of China State Control of the Internet in China," *Amnesty International* 2002. www.amnesty.org

Kofi A. Annan   "Democracy as an International Issue," *Global Governance*, April 1, 2002.

Paula J. Dobriansky   "Shining a Light: U.S. Efforts to Strengthen Democracy Worldwide," *U.S. Foreign Policy Agenda*, August 2003.

Johanni Hari   "George Bush's Talk of Spreading Freedom and Democracy Is a Sugar-Coated Lie," *Independent*, January 21, 2005.

Thom Hartmann   "When Democracy Failed: The Warnings of History," *CommonDreams.org*, March 16, 2003. www.commondreams.org

Fred Hiatt   "Democracy in Trouble: Now We Understand That It's Not Inevitable," *Washington Post*, September 20, 2004.

Eric J. Hobsbawm   "Spreading Democracy: The World's Most Dangerous Ideas," *Foreign Policy*, September/October 2004.

David Lowe   "Expanding Democracy Around the World: Prospects and Challenges," Address to the Savannah Council on World Affairs, September 18, 2003. www.ned.org

Ilana Mercer   "Exporting Democracy," *WorldNetDaily.com*, 2003. www.wnd.com

Gilberto Meza   "Disillusioned with Democracy? Authoritarianism Looks Appealing in Light of Democratic Disappointments," *Business Mexico*, November 1, 2004.

Branko Milanovic   "Democracy and Income Inequality: An Empirical Analysis," *Social Science Research Network Electronic Library*, January 2001. http://papers.ssrn.com

Eric Mink   "Setting a Bad Example: President Bush Talks a Lot About Spreading Democracy but He's Not Practicing What He Preaches Overseas," *St. Louis Post-Dispatch*, June 8, 2005.

Daniel M. Nelson	"Dangerous Assumptions: The U.S. Is Assuming That Democracy Will Take Root in Central Europe," *Bulletin of the Atomic Scientists*, July 1, 2000.
Jonathan Rauch	"Democracy Everywhere? What a Nutty Idea," *National Journal*, May 21, 2005.
Frederick C. Risinger	"Thomas Jefferson, the Internet, and the Future of American Democracy," *Social Education*, September 1, 2000.
Michel Rocard	"Democracy Is Spreading, Believe It," *Daily Star*, August 9, 2004.
Donald B. Schulz	"The Growing Threat to Democracy in Latin America," *Parameters*, March 22, 2001.

CHAPTER 2

What Should Be the Relationship Between Religion and Democracy?

Chapter Preface

Understanding the role that religion plays in democracies can be challenging, especially when the democracy under study is America. On the one hand, America's founders created a country without an official religion. On the other hand, these same men proclaimed the importance of religious faith to the success of their new nation. As a brief examination of several events in U.S. history illustrates, this apparent contradiction lies at the center of American political life.

The Europeans who first settled in North America were fleeing religious persecution in their home nations. Notwithstanding this fact, many still believed there should be a single official religion in their new home. For example, Maryland was founded for Catholics. Puritans in Massachusetts Bay believed that all laws had to be based on "God's law," and they drove Calvinists out of the colony.

Roger Williams, a Puritan minister objected to these actions. He wrote in 1644, "God requireth not a uniformity of religion to be enacted and enforced in any civil state; which enforced uniformity (sooner or later) is the greatest occasion of civil war, ravishing of conscience, persecution of Christ Jesus in his servants, and of the hypocrisy and destruction of millions of souls." Williams was banished by the Puritans and went on to found Rhode Island, the first state without an official religion. Williams's insistence on freedom of religion inspired others—including the founding fathers—to question the role religion should play in political life.

The desire to protect religious freedom and to recognize the fact that people of many different faiths lived in America motivated the founding fathers to include in the Constitution two important provisions regarding religion. Article VI states that "no religious test shall ever be required as a qualification to any office or public trust under the United States." Charles Haynes, senior scholar at the First Amendment Center, has observed, "With this bold stroke, the framers broke with European tradition and opened public office in the federal government to people of any faith and no faith." The other important provision is the First Amendment to the U.S. Constitution, which states that "Congress shall make no law respecting an establishment of religion, or prohibiting the free exercise thereof." Thomas Jefferson, in an 1802 letter to the Danbury Baptist Association, stated that this provision of the Constitution built "a wall of separation between church and state."

Although the founders protected religious freedom by creating a government without an official religion, they also made public statements about the importance of religious faith to their new nation. Thomas Jefferson said in *Notes on the State of Virginia (1781–1785)*, "Can the liberties of a nation be thought secure when we have removed their only firm basis, a conviction in the minds of the people that these liberties are a gift of God?" George Washington, in his farewell address after his second term as president, stated to Congress, "Of all the dispositions and habits, which lead to political prosperity, Religion and Morality are indispensable supports. . . . Let us with caution indulge the supposition, that morality can be maintained without religion. Whatever may be conceded to the influence of refined education on minds of peculiar structure, reason and experience both forbid us to expect, that national morality can prevail in exclusion of religious principle."

How to maintain religious freedom while acknowledging the importance of faith remains a challenge for the world's democracies. The authors in this chapter debate the proper role of religion in democracy and whether politicians should talk about their own religious beliefs. The authors also debate whether democracy is possible in Islamic countries.

*"The constitutional authority for
'separation' in church-state separation
has . . . historical foundations."*

Democracy Is Based on Secular Principles

Clark Moeller

In this viewpoint Clark Moeller, a founder and former president of the Pennsylvania Alliance for Democracy, argues that the founders created a secular democracy. Moeller says separation of church and state was an important consideration leading to adoption of the First Amendment. The phrase "separation of church and state," he says, has become part of our common language. He argues that calling America a Christian nation makes little sense because many Americans are not self-proclaimed Christians and those who are hold conflicting beliefs. The complete article from which this viewpoint was excerpted, and the citations for all quotes and additional supporting documentation, can be found in the appendix of Clark Moeller's *Church-State Separation: A Keystone for Peace*, 2004, at www.padnet.org/CSSmoeller2.pdf.

As you read, consider the following questions:

1. What two writers does Moeller quote to support his contention that the idea of civil government being separate from proselytizing clergy was not a new idea in the 1790s?
2. What did Ulysses S. Grant say about church-state separation during his presidential campaign, according to Moeller?

Three common criticisms of church-state separation include the complaints that the meaning of the Establishment Clause in the First Amendment of the Constitution of the United States does not imply the concept of separation of church from state; none of the separation phrases such as 'church-state separation' or 'wall of separation' are found in the language of the First Amendment; and America is a Christian nation and has been since its founding in 1778.

The first criticism claims that church-state separation is not what is meant by the first part of the First Amendment:, "Congress shall make no law respecting an establishment of religion, or prohibiting the free exercise thereof";

This claim fails the historical test. The constitutional authority for 'separation' in church-state separation has two historical foundations. First, the concept of keeping religion separate from the mundane and morally compromised machinations of politics in government in order to protect the purity of religion has a long theological tradition. Roger Williams, the founder of the Rhode Island colony, took this position in his *Queries of Highest Consideration* (1644) and in his arguments with the civil authorities of the Massachusetts Bay Company.

Second, the idea that civil government should be separate from proselytizing clergy and the political aspirations of ecclesiastical authorities was not a new idea in the 1790s. John Locke supported this concept of separation. He was one of the most widely read political theorists of his day, and his writings had a significant influence on the thinking of the founders of this country. In regard to the authority of the clergy, Locke wrote in 1688, ". . . it [the ecclesiastical authority] ought to be confined within the bounds of the church, nor can it in any manner be extended to civil affairs, because the church itself is a thing absolutely separate and distinct from the commonwealth. The boundaries on both sides are fixed and immovable." Another writer with a perspective similar to Locke's was Marquis de Condorcet, a French intellectual whom Thomas Jefferson most likely read when he was in France as the United States' representative from 1785 to 1789. In 1786, Condorcet wrote, "The interest of the princes was not to seek to regulate religion, but to separate religion from the state, to leave to the priests the freedom of sacraments, censures, ecclesiastical functions; but not to give any civil effect to any of their decisions, not to give them any influence over marriages or over birth or death certificates; not to allow them to intervene in any civil or political acts. . . ."

Both reasons for separation, the state from religious institutions as Williams would have it, and clergy from the state as Condorcet and Locke argued, were reflected in the writings of important founders of our government.

"For Madison and Jefferson, freedom of conscience meant the freedom to exercise religious liberty [as an individual]—to worship or not, to support a church or not, to profess belief or disbelief—without suffering civil penalties or incapacity. It had nothing to do with a right to choose one's beliefs," because, according to Jefferson, "the opinion and beliefs of men depend not on their own will, but follow involuntarily the evidence proposed to their own minds." According to Jefferson and Madison, this goal for religious freedom was best achieved by the means of church-state separation. For example, James Madison, the architect of the Constitution, wrote in 1785 that religion is ". . . not within the cognizance of civil government. . . . The general government is proscribed from interfering, in any manner whatever, in matters respecting religion." As the First Amendment scholar Leonard Levy notes, Madison "led the fight in Virginia against the 'general assessment' bill of 1784, which would have imposed taxes to subsidize religion. . . . Madison opposed . . . any kind of establishment of religion, no matter how inclusive or exclusive. . . . He shared Jefferson's belief in a high wall of separation. Madison spoke of a 'perfect separation' and believed that 'religion and Government will exist in greater purity, without . . . the aid of government.'"

In 1789, George Washington wrote that he ". . . would labor zealously . . . to establish effectual barriers against the horrors of spiritual tyranny, and every species of religious persecution." Also in 1789, the Constitution of the United States was adopted with no reference to God, a radical act for the day, that separated any suggestion of religious authority from the foundational document of the United

States government. Finally, various drafts for the wording for the First Amendment were debated by Congress before the proposed draft was sent to the states for ratifications in 1789. All 13 state legislatures debated the wording of the First Amendment before it became part of the Constitution on December 15, 1791.

In 1797, another Founder President John Adams concluded the "Treaty of Peace and Friendship between the United States of America and the Bey and Subjects of Tripoli, which stated, "As the Government of the United States . . . is not in any sense founded on the Christian religion—as it has in itself no character of enmity against the laws, religion, or tranquillity of Musselmen [sic]—and as the said States never have entered into any war or act of hostility against any Mehomitan [sic] nation, it is declared by the parties that no pretext arising from religious opinions shall ever produce an interruption of the harmony existing between the two countries." This treaty was unanimously approved by the United States Senate.

A second criticism of church-state separation is that none of the phrases 'church-state separation,' 'separation of church and state,' or 'wall of separation' appear in the Constitution of the United States. If this objection is intended to be taken seriously, its advocates have the epistemological burden of explaining how a person understands the meaning of what others say. Our common understanding of what words mean is one of the primary ways by which we affirm, dispute, or reconcile our observations with the reported perceptions of others. The phrase 'wall of separation' is a metaphor which expresses in just three words the purpose of the Establishment Clause. Common synonyms of this include 'church-state separation' and 'separation of church and state.'

A variation of the complaint that the term 'church-state separation' does not appear in the Constitution was offered by the former House Speaker Newt Gingrich who argued, "You can't find a single line in the Constitution on secularism." But the definition of secularism according to Webster's is, "the belief that religion and ecclesiastical affairs should not enter into the functions of the state, esp. into public education," which is exactly what the Constitution proscribes in the Establishment Clause of the First Amendment, "Congress shall make no laws respecting religion;" and this intent is reinforced by the lack of any reference to the term God or any term suggesting a deity in the Constitution.

How words are used in daily life is the criterion lexicographers employ to determine the meaning of words and phrases. By this criterion, the 'church-state separation' phrase has entered the English language as an accepted and widely understood phrase expressing the intent of the Establishment Clause in the First Amendment of the Constitution of the United States.

In 1875, both the Republican and Democratic political parties adopted political planks endorsing church-state separation for their presidential campaigns. Ulysses S. Grant supported this position by saying, "Keep the church and the state forever separate." In 1876, the U.S. House of Representatives passed the Blaine amendment 109 to 7 to amend the Constitution in order to make the concept of church-state separation more explicit, and to have it apply to the states as well as the relationship between the Federal government and religions. This proposed amendment failed in the Senate by only two votes. However, by then many states, such as Pennsylvania, had adopted language providing for church-state separation in their state constitutions. Seventy seven years later, in 1952, Congress approved the constitution of Puerto Rico which includes the phrase "complete separation of church and state."

For two centuries, the language of church-state separation has been and continues to be used in newspapers and books. On November 18, 2002, *The New York Times* reported, "[Federal] Judge Thompson issued a 93-page opinion today, saying Justice Moore had violated the separation between church and state." The meaning of these phrases 'church-state separation,' 'separation of church and state,' or 'wall of separation' are so well established that these terms are used in book indexes to cross-reference subject matter. *The Columbia Encyclopedia* (1963) defined separation of church and state on page 416. Similar language is used in *Barrett's World Christian Encyclopedia: a Comparative Study of Churches and Religions in the Modern World AD 1900–2000.*

The index of Robert Wuthnow's authoritative, two-volume *The Encyclopedia of Politics and Religion*, includes "Separation of church and state."

The durability of the language of separation since 1802, when President Jefferson proclaimed a "wall of separation," is testimony to the productive utility that these phrases have had in summarizing in a few words the meaning of the Establishment Clause.

Why Government Cannot Endorse Religion

The Supreme Court's historic decisions concerning religion in the public square, including the public schools, have never sought to establish irreligion in America, but rather have sought to protect the right of all to freely exercise their own religion, free from government coercion or interference. The best guarantee of the free exercise of religion has been the requirement that the government refrains from being an advocate of religion, thereby preventing any advancement or endorsement of any kind of religious doctrine. And by keeping the government out of every aspect of religion's business, Americans have ensured the sanctity of their religious practices. As Justice [Sandra Day] O'Connor noted in her concurring opinion in *County of Allegheny* (1989), "We live in a pluralistic society. Our citizens come from diverse religious traditions, or adhere to no particular religious beliefs at all. If government is to be neutral in matters of religion, rather than showing either favoritism or disapproval towards citizens based on their personal religious choices, government cannot endorse the religious practices and beliefs of some citizens without sending a clear message to non-adherents that they are outsiders or less than full members of the political community."

Derek H. Davis, *Journal of Church and State*, September 22, 2004.

Finally, some claim that "America is a Christian nation" and therefore there is no such thing as church-state separation. To respond to this claim I will start with a few definitions. A "nation" is defined by its form of government and the characteristics of its legal system. The seminal event of 1787 that distinguished the newly formed "nation" of the United States from all preceding and existing nations of that era was the adoption by the Continental Congress of a secular constitution, with no mention of God, and the Constitution explicitly states in Article VI, Clause 3: ". . . no religious test shall ever be required as a qualification to any office or public trust under the United States." The Constitution and the adoption of the First Amendment in 1791, were watershed events in the history of world politics; a new paradigm of government was created that had no formal or legal connection to organized religion. As a result, the "nation" of the United States is, and has always been, secular by constitutional definition. Therefore, our nation is not a Christian theocracy as suggested by the statement "America is a Christian nation."

Second, perhaps some critics of church-state separation assume that the population of this secular nation is Christian to such an extent that America might fairly be characterized as a "Christian" country. This raises the two questions: how is "Christian" defined, that is, what set of beliefs are common to Christians and how do we determine if a person is Christian? Answers to these will help us determine whether there is a reasonable justification for claiming "America is a Christian nation?"

As to the first question, there appears to be little agreement about which beliefs define a Christian. Today, some self-identified Christians dismiss the validity or relevance of central Christian doctrines, such as being born in sin, the importance of forgiveness, or even the essential role of Christ. For example, in a 2000 *New York Times* survey, 73% of Americans disagree that we are born in sin. Although for many forgiveness is a defining attribute of Christianity, the four Gospels do not consistently support forgiveness as a virtue.

"There is a moral majority in America," reports Alan Wolfe, director of the Boisi Center for Religion and American Public Life at Boston College. "It just happens to be one that wants to make up its own mind." For example, self-proclaimed Christians are on both sides of such important issues as the place of women in society, contraception, a woman's right to choose abortion, medically assisted suicide, prayer in public schools, teaching evolution in public schools, gay and women clergy, and equal civil rights for gays.

Such differences are not limited to the laity. In 1987, only

5% of Episcopalian clergy agreed that ". . . the Scriptures are the inspired and inerrant Word of God in faith, history, and secular matters," compared to 33% of American Baptist clergy, according to a poll conducted by Jeffery Hadden of 10,000 American clergy. In 2000, "the 8.4 million-member United Methodist Church declared that Mormonism [with 11 million members] 'by self-definition, does not fit within the bounds of the historic, apostolic tradition of the Christian faith.'" Such definitional distinctions further compromise the claim that "America is a Christian nation."

Given the wide range of conflicting religious beliefs held by self-identified Christians and the theological chasm separating many Christian denominations, it is difficult to imagine that there is or will ever be a consensus among Christians about what the phrase "America is a 'Christian' nation" means.

The second question was how do we determine if a person is Christian. In 1956, about 80% of the U.S. population surveyed claimed some religious identity or affiliation such as Jewish, Presbyterian, or Catholic. Most self-identified as Christian. However, church records indicated that only 62% of the adult population were members of a congregation, and less than that, 45%, attended church. Attendance dropped to about 35% nationally by 1995, and in a survey of New York City residents in 2000, 25% reported they attended a house of worship.

If the old maxim "actions speak louder than words" has any merit, church attendance is the most compelling evidence of traditional religious commitment. The large disparities between reported religious self-identity, church membership, and church attendance further weakens the claim that "America is a Christian nation."

A variation of the "America is a Christian nation" claim is the assertion that colonial Americans were Christian at the time when the United States was founded. However, in 1776, only 17% of Americans were members of any church as compared to about 60% today. If the pattern of church-going in 1776 was similar to that of today then only 35% of the 17%, who were church members, actually attended church in 1776. To say that "America was a Christian nation" in 1776 has little factual foundation.

The attitude reflected in the claim that "America is a Christian nation" is at odds with the sentiment of 83% of Americans who agree that ". . . there are many different religious truths and we ought to be tolerant of all of them"; and it conflicts with the long-term, broad, public support for church-state separation. Americans do not want to give up their democracy for a fundamentalist, theocratic vision of the United States. That was true in 1791 when the First Amendment was adopted, and it continues to be the case today.

| "*The Founders pointed out that only a 'moral' and 'God-fearing' people could meet the demands of individual freedom.*"

Democracy Is Based on Religious Principles

Bill O'Reilly

Bill O'Reilly argues in the following viewpoint that the concept of separation of church and state is faulty. He contends that the success of American democracy depends upon citizens being moral and God-fearing. He claims that lawsuits attempting to prevent religion being referred to in the public sphere run counter to the purposes of the Founding Fathers, who believed that religion was essential to democracy. American democracy, which restricts the powers of government to rule the people, depends on American citizens governing themselves according to the Ten Commandments, O'Reilly asserts. Bill O'Reilly is a journalist, author, and host of "The O'Reilly Factor," a TV news show on the Fox network.

As you read, consider the following questions:

1. According to the author, if a society does not fear God, upon what does it rely for moral guidance?
2. Who called the Constitution "a mere thing of wax in the hands of the judiciary, which they may twist and shape into any form they please"?
3. What fraction of Americans think school prayer should be permitted?

Bill O'Reilly, *Who's Looking Out for You?* New York: Broadway Books, 2003. Copyright © 2003 by Bill O'Reilly. Reproduced by permission of Broadway Books, a division of Random House, Inc.

In our personal lives, we do actually enjoy full freedom of religion in this country. But publicly that is no longer so in America. Because of the rise of secularism, a philosophy that argues there is no room for spirituality in the public arena, religious expression in public is under pressure from some in the media and, of course, from the intolerant secularists who hold power in many different quarters. They are *definitely* not looking out for you.

One of the biggest frauds ever foisted upon the American people is the issue of separation of church and state. The American Civil Liberties Union, along with legal secularists like Supreme Court justices Ruth Bader Ginsburg and John Paul Stevens, are using the Constitution to bludgeon any form of public spirituality. This insidious strategy goes against everything the Founding Fathers hoped to achieve in forming a free, humane society.

I said "fraud," and I meant it. Let's look at some historical facts. There is no question that Benjamin Franklin, Thomas Jefferson, James Madison, and most of the other framers encouraged spirituality in our public discourse. Letters written by these great men show that they believed social stability could be achieved only by a people who embraced a moral God. Time after time in debating the future of America, the Founders pointed out that only a "moral" and "God-fearing" people could meet the demands of individual freedom. That makes perfect sense, because a society that has no fear of God relies solely on civil authority for guidance. But that guidance can and has broken down. All great philosophers, even the atheists, realized that one of the essential attributes of a civilized people is a belief that good will be rewarded and evil will be punished.

In 1781, Jefferson said the following words, which are engraved on the Jefferson Memorial in Washington: "God who gave us life gave us liberty. Can the liberties of a nation be secure when we have removed a conviction that these liberties are the gift of God?"

"Keep God in the Public Arena"

I wonder what Jefferson would think of the ruling by the Ninth Circuit Court of Appeals in California that the word

God is unconstitutional in the Pledge of Allegiance. I also wonder what ol' Tom would think of the American Civil Liberties Union suing school districts all over the country to ban the use of the word God in school-sanctioned speech. Here's how ridiculous this whole thing is: At McKinley High School in Honolulu, an official school poem has been recited on ceremonial occasions since *1927*. One of the lines mentions a love for God. After the ACLU threatened a lawsuit, that poem was banned from public recitation, a seventy-five-year tradition dissolved within a few weeks.

Asay. © 2002 by Creators Syndicate, Inc. Reproduced by permission.

This is tragic insanity. To any intellectually honest person, it is apparent that the Founders wanted very much to keep God in the public arena, even uppermost in the thoughts of the populace. What the Founders *did not* want was any one religion *imposed* by the government. Jefferson, and Madison in particular, were suspicious of organized religion and of some of the zealots who assumed power in faith-based organizations. But the Founders kept it simple: All law-abiding religions were allowed to practice, but the government would not favor any one above another.

At the same time, Jefferson in his wisdom predicted that some of the things he and the others wanted for the new country would eventually come under fire. On September 6, 1819, he wrote: "The Constitution . . . is a mere thing of wax in the hands of the judiciary, which they may twist and shape into any form they please."

How prophetic is that? Right now we have well-funded and extremely litigious groups of anti-spirituality people running wild in the U.S.A., and a number of judges are in their pockets. Led by the incredibly vicious ACLU, they are suing towns, school boards, states, and municipalities to wipe out any public displays relating to heavenly matters.

The ACLU Is Wrong

In addition to the Hawaii case, there have been dozens of other disturbing developments: In Georgia, the ACLU sued to get the words *Christmas holiday* taken off a school district's calendar, the antispirituality fanatics demanding the words *winter holiday* be substituted. But President [Ulysses S.] Grant did not sign legislation making "winter holiday" a federal day off. No, he signed into law the "Christmas holiday." Nevertheless, the ACLU's bullying legal tactics succeeded in that case.

In Alabama, civil libertarians sued to get the Ten Commandments removed from a state courtroom. They won. You know about the Pledge of Allegiance suit in California, and I could give you hundreds of other examples. In New Jersey, the secularists even stopped schoolkids from seeing *A Christmas Carol*, based upon the Charles Dickens novel. The kids went to see some cartoon instead.

And the most insane incident of all occurred in New Mexico, where secularists demanded that the town of Las Cruces change its name. Las Cruces means "the cross." (It's still Las Cruces. And the upstate New York town of Fishkill is still called that despite the efforts of animal rights crazies to have it legally changed.)

What must Benjamin Franklin think as he looks down from Heaven? In 1787, Franklin delivered a stirring speech at the Constitutional Convention in which he said: "I therefore beg leave to move—that henceforth, prayers imploring

the assistance of Heaven and its blessing on our delibera-
tions, be held in this Assembly every morning before we
proceed to business, and that one or more of the clergy of
this city be requested to officiate in that service."

Religion and Liberty Are Intimately Connected

George Washington, America's first president, wrote, "I am
sure there never was a people who had more reason to ac-
knowledge a divine interposition in their affairs, than those
of the U.S. I should be pained to believe . . . that they failed
to consider the omnipotence of God, who is alone able to
protect them."

The nation's second president, John Adams, added, "Our
Constitution was designed for a moral and religious people
only. It is wholly inadequate for any other." By this, Adams
did not mean that the Constitution was meant for people of
any specific faith. He opposed religious tests for public office, as do I and most Americans. The point Adams made was
far more profound. He meant that, to create a nation where
government was small, limited, and confined to enumerated
functions, one must have a virtuous citizenry animated by
faith in God and moral values.

The nation's founders possessed a view of the world and government that necessarily presupposed a people obedient to
an internalized code of conduct—based upon that first, and
in my mind still the best, code of law found in the books of
Moses—that made a large central government superfluous.
It was this view that French statesman Alexis de Tocqueville
wrote about in the early 19th century: "The Americans com-
bine the notions of [religion] and liberty so intimately in
their minds, that it is impossible to make them conceive of
one without the other."

Ralph Reed, "Democracy and Religion Are Not Incompatible," *USA Today*,
July 1, 1997.

Prayers? Before a public debate? Clergy? Some Supreme
Court justices are gagging on their gavels. And those jurists
must really hate 1787, because also in that year the North-
west Ordinance was passed to govern the territories not yet
admitted into the Union. Article III of that ordinance states:
"Religion, morality, and knowledge being necessary to good
government and the happiness of mankind, schools, and the

means of education shall be forever encouraged."

Forever? Religion? Schools? Holy water, Batman! Does this mean that the media and the secularist judges and the intrusively dishonest ACLU have all lied to us? That's exactly what it means, Robin.

The Ten Commandments

Let's take a look at those Ten Commandments. Boy, the federal courts don't want you to see those on any government property, no way. But wait, there's a signpost up ahead. It was written by James Madison, the guiding force behind the language of the Constitution. Said Madison: "We have staked the whole future of American civilization, not upon the power of government, far from it. We have staked the future of all of our political institutions upon the capacity of mankind for self-government; upon the capacity of each and all of us to govern ourselves, to control ourselves, to sustain ourselves according to THE TEN COMMANDMENTS." (My emphasis.)

President Madison knew, as did all his founding brothers, that a precise moral code was necessary to set boundaries for everyday life. Ruth Bader Ginsburg and her pals want to erase those boundaries and allow those in power to govern solely by manmade law. But that is impossible. No government can police individual behavior on a massive scale. Either a society has morals or it turns into the Mongol hordes. The way the U.S.A. is going, you might want to start taking riding lessons.

It should be abundantly clear that the antispirituality forces in this country are on a tear. The trend began in June 2000, when a 6-to-3 Supreme Court decision held that a student in a Texas public school violated the Constitution by offering a public prayer before a football game. Interestingly, the entire student body in the school had voted on the student who would deliver the prayer. It was considered a great honor.

Writing for the majority, Justice John Paul Stevens opined in part, "School sponsorship of a religious message is impermissible." Yet a national poll on the situation found that two out of three Americans thought that the prayer should be permitted.

Chief Justice William Rehnquist [who died in 2005], one of the three dissenting judges, summed up the situation this way: "Even more disturbing than its holding is the tone of the court's opinion; it bristles with hostility to all things religious in public life."

That is absolutely true. In every debate about public spirituality, the secularists spin the issue and equate God with the legal concept of religion. The two are separate, and here's some legal proof. God is a spiritual being. Witches and Wiccans are recognized religious groups. They reject God.

Judeo-Christian Philosophy

The United States was founded on Judeo-Christian *philosophy*, not a particular religion. As Madison pointed out, in order for a just society to exist, Americans must behave according to an established moral code, and they chose the Ten Commandments as a good model. That is the logic of the situation. A philosophy that citizens must love and fear a higher power and love their neighbors as themselves encourages civility on a mass scale. As I mentioned, the Founders knew America would never survive the challenges of freedom if spirituality was not a part of the nation's fabric.

Yet the spirituality and philosophy of the Founding Fathers have now been beaten to a pulp by the hyperaggressive forces of the secular opposition. They have waged a successful campaign to convince millions of Americans that public spirituality is "noninclusive" and therefore offensive. They have succeeded mightily in burying the true tenor of this country: That there *is* a right and wrong. That everyone is entitled to pursue happiness while receiving the protection of an effective and responsible federal government that understands the intent of the Constitution and those who forged it.

But why have the secularists launched their jihad [holy war]? Well, the primary reason is that they do not want personal conduct to be judged. That's what this holy war is all about. If spirituality is encouraged in the public arena, then questions about violent crime, corrupting media products, drug use, abortion, sexual behavior, conspicuous consumption, irresponsible parental conduct, and a myriad of other personal issues will be raised. Above all, the secularists do not want that. They want a moral free-fire zone in the U.S.A., where consenting adults can do just about anything in the name of personal freedom. It is not an accident or a coincidence that as moral imperatives have broken down, the number of American children born out of wedlock has skyrocketed in the past decade. And that is the primary cause of poverty and crime. . . .

From their experiences in Europe, the Founding Fathers knew that a lax approach to personal behavior leads to decadence and decay. The Founders wanted moral boundaries and standards of behavior set at the local level. They did not want the excesses of England under the Hanovers or France under Louis XVI.

But tyrant Louis would love secular America here in the early part of the twenty-first century. Our dismissal of spirituality in the public schools and the embracing of secular values and thought throughout society would have greatly cheered mad King George III as well as loopy Louis and his greedy wife, Marie Antoinette. But America is paying a heavy price for letting the good times roll, a price seen most vividly in the behavior of children and especially public high school students.

> *"The claim that conscience can or should be ignored in specific policy areas is disingenuous. . . . Moral considerations of some sort come into play in every policy decision."*

Politicians Should Voice Their Religious Convictions

Jordan Ballor

In this viewpoint Jordan Ballor argues that politicians should craft public policies in accordance with their religions faith. Ballor maintains that instead of distancing moral convictions from political debates, in order to curry public opinion, politicians should frankly engage in religious and political discussion. Religious convictions are important to an honest exercise of conscience and are therefore essential to democracy, he claims. Ballor is an associate editor with the Acton Institute for the Study of Religion & Liberty.

As you read, consider the following questions:

1. What historic example of injustice in the United States that was supported by a majority does the author give?
2. According to a poll cited by the author, what percentage of Americans believe it is important for a president to believe in God and be deeply religious?
3. Who said that legislators cannot approve laws contrary to "the highest values of the human person and proceeding in the last analysis from God, the Supreme Legislator"?

Jordan Ballor, "Private Faith and Public Politics," www.acton.org, March 17, 2004. Copyright © 2004 by the Acton Institute. Reproduced by permission.

[A 2004] poll revealed that most Americans have a favorable view of religion in the political arena. An O'Leary Report/Zogby International Values poll showed that nearly 60 percent of Americans "say it's important for a president to believe in God and be deeply religious." More evidence that, at least as far as the poll data shows, Americans take their religion seriously. . . .

John F. Kennedy, campaigning in 1960 to become the nation's first Catholic president, famously promised the Greater Houston Ministerial Alliance that he would follow his own conscience, not the Vatican's. "I do not speak for my church on public matters—and the church does not speak for me," Kennedy said.

But must faith remain a private matter for elected officials? If not, how then should political leaders of faith inform their decision-making while doing justice to the plurality of religious beliefs among their constituencies? In a representative democracy like the United States, some feel that their religious convictions should not inform or determine their policy decisions, out of deference for differing views among the electorate. But the claim that conscience can or should be ignored in specific policy areas is disingenuous, however. Moral considerations of some sort come into play in every policy decision. Political leaders tend to distance their moral convictions from the debate in favor of public opinion only when it is politically expedient.

True statesmen are not merely mouthpieces for opinion polls. British historian Lord Acton recognized that the will of the majority could be and often is just as tyrannical as the will of a monarch, and in some cases more dangerous because the error has the support of the masses. Thus he observes, "It is bad to be oppressed by a minority, but it is worse to be oppressed by a majority," and, "The will of the people cannot make just that which is unjust." These statements speak to the biblical reality confessed by the apostles, "We must obey God rather than human beings!"

In the United States we have compelling historical and contemporary examples of the majority siding with what were, in retrospect, clear-cut cases of injustice. The legalization and promotion of slavery by governments are a prime

Expressions of Religious Faith and Prayer by . . .

	Political leaders %	G.W. Bush %
Too little	41	11
Too much	21	14
Right amount	29	62
Don't know	9	13
	100	100

Note: chart shows what percentage of Americans express concern about the use of religious rhetoric by political leaders.

"Religion and Politics: Contention and Consensus," Pew Forum on Religion and Public Life, July 2003. http://pewforum.org.

example, and stand as a sharp rebuke to elected officials who think they ought simply to represent the people, without regard to their own conscience. Today, there are a number of hotly contentious issues—such as abortion, stem cell research and, now, marriage—whose partisans often make appeals based on poll data. Our elected officials follow the shifting temper of the electorate with rapt attention. But is this how we ask our elected officials to lead?

Duty to Link Faith and Policy

Pope John Paul II recently reiterated the necessary link between faith and public policy. Politicians have a duty to bring their faith to bear in their public life. "I consider it opportune to recall that the legislator, and the Catholic legislator in particular, cannot contribute to the formulation or approval of laws contrary to 'the primary and essential norms that regulate moral life,' the expressions of the highest values of the human person and proceeding in the last analysis from God, the Supreme Legislator," the Pope said.

Politicians do themselves and those they represent no justice by rigidly separating out their religious convictions from their policy decisions. Neither is the electorate advantaged by the omission of authentic religious discussion and engagement of political issues.

Of course simply invoking faith superficially for any issue

does not constitute a valid way of meeting these obligations. A heartfelt desire to help the poor, for example, is not enough. Policymaking also requires sound economic thinking and a discernment of the moral underpinnings of competing economic systems. The Bible can and has been claimed for any number of hateful and destructive programs, both political and social. It is in the particular engagement of faith and public duty that prayer and discernment play key roles.

Political leaders of all faiths must bring their respective traditions to bear on their decisions. This is an honest exercise of conscience, and one best managed in a spirit of tolerance and respect. To do otherwise is to commit an act of moral cowardice. In an age when so many are echoing Pontius Pilate's confused question, "What is truth?" Too many political leaders have settled on an inadequate answer: the will of the people (and the pollsters).

> *"The idea that politicians should keep
> their religious faith private may seem
> outrageously intolerant. But is it not
> equally outrageous that, on today's political
> scene, a secularist figure cannot express his
> views honestly without committing career
> suicide?"*

Politicians Should Not Voice Their Religious Convictions

Cathy Young

Cathy Young argues that bringing religion into the public square penalizes secularist politicians. She contends that when certain segments of the population—atheists and secularists—are denied access to political power, democracy suffers. Young also contends that justifying public policies by invoking God's name suggests that non-believers are not true Americans, reducing a large percentage of Americans to political pariahs. Young is a columnist for the *Boston Globe*.

As you read, consider the following questions:

1. What effect did Howard Dean say that religion had on his public policy views?
2. How does the U.S. Constitution address religious qualifications for public office?
3. What fraction of Americans do not consider religion very important in their lives?

Cathy Young, "Beyond Belief: When Will Secularism Be Allowed in the Public Square?" *Reason*, October 1, 2004. Copyright © 2004 by the Reason Foundation, 3415 S. Sepulveda Blvd., Suite 400, Los Angeles, CA 90034, www.reason.com. Reproduced by permission.

When John F. Kennedy ran for President in 1960, his Roman Catholic faith was widely viewed as a stumbling block to his campaign. Many voters feared that Catholic politicians would look to the Vatican for guidance, putting their loyalty to the Church above their obligations to the American people.

Kennedy responded by reiterating his absolute commitment to the separation of church and state. In a September 1960 address to the Greater Houston Ministerial Association, he declared his belief in "an America where . . . no Catholic prelate would tell the president [should he be Catholic] how to act."

Fast-forward 44 years to the presidential campaign of another Catholic Democrat from Massachusetts, Sen. John Kerry. This time around, the charge [was] that he is insufficiently loyal to the Catholic Church.

Religion in the 2004 Presidential Campaign

In June 2004, the Los Angeles based Catholic lawyer Mark Balestrieri filed heresy charges against Kerry with the Boston Archdiocese, asking that he be excommunicated because of his support for legal abortion. Around the same time, Pope John Paul II's [then] doctrinal adviser, Cardinal [Joseph] Ratzinger[1] sent a memo to the U.S. Conference of Catholic Bishops stating that politicians who support abortion rights should be denied communion. Four American bishops already had said they would deny Kerry communion.

Some commentators—including several conservatives, such as *The Weekly Standard*'s Terry Eastland—noted that such tactics could backfire. But the controversy was generally seen as a liability and an embarrassment for Kerry. In his speech accepting the Democratic nomination at his party's convention in July [2004], Kerry asserted that he did not wear his faith on his sleeve, yet much of his speech was crafted in religious terms.

Religion in politics has come a long way since 1960.

Kerry is not the first Democratic candidate to have a religion problem this campaign. The former front-runner,

1. Cardinal Ratzinger became Pope Benedict XVI in 2005.

Howard Dean, was labeled too secular to be electable. A January 2004 cover story by Franklin Foer in *The New Republic* declared that Dean would have trouble shedding the "liberal" image—less because of his politics than because he was "one of the most secular candidates to run for president in modern history." (Dean, an Episcopalian turned Congregationalist, had openly said that he didn't go to church often and that religion didn't inform his public policy views.)

Other publications picked up on this theme. In a particularly bizarre moment, an interview with Dean by *Newsweek*'s Howard Fineman abruptly turned from various policy issues to the question, "Do you see Jesus Christ as the son of God and believe in him as the route to salvation and eternal life?"

It's hard to tell whether the meteoric fall of Dean's candidacy had anything to do with his perceived secularism—or, for that matter, with his clumsy attempt to reinvent himself as a man of faith. Nonetheless, few would disagree with Foer's statement, "One day, a truly secular candidate might be able to run for president without suffering at the polls. But that day won't be soon."

"Tide of Religiosity"

Article VI of the U.S. Constitution explicitly states that "no religious test shall ever be required as a qualification to any office or public trust." But formal tests are one thing, voter preferences another; no one can keep the people from imposing a religious litmus test on candidates. Today that litmus test is not membership in a particular religion but religiosity in general—though it's hard to tell how the public would react to a Muslim or a Hindu candidate. In a 2000 Pew Research Center poll, 70 percent of Americans said that they wanted a presidential candidate to be religious.

The prominence of religion in the Bush White House makes secularist liberals profoundly nervous. Four of the six blurbs on the back of Susan Jacoby's *Freethinkers: A History of American Secularism*, published in May 2004, refer directly or indirectly to the Bush presidency—what [historian] Arthur Schlesinger Jr. called, in his blurb, "the tide of religiosity engulfing a once secular republic."

The real picture, as usual, is more complex. Indeed, Jacoby's fascinating if flawed history demonstrates that religiosity and secularism have always been competing strains in American public life. In a cyclical pattern, relatively secular periods have been followed by religious upsurges.

Making Political Points

[S]ome candidates and their zealous supporters make speeches or sales pitches with a religious flavor that frequently have less to do with God than with getting votes or making political points.

Robert King, *St. Petersburg Times*, February 2, 2004. www.sptimes.com.

There is no question that religion and politics are entangled today in ways that would have been unthinkable in 1960. But blaming this solely on the right is disingenuous. Jimmy Carter was the first modern president to wear his faith on his sleeve. In 2000 [presidential candidate] Al Gore claimed that "What would Jesus do?" was his guide to making policy, while his running mate, Joe Lieberman, talked of renewing "the dedication of our nation and ourselves to God and God's purpose."

Religion on the Left

Critics of Christian conservatives are often blind to it, but religion and politics mix freely on the left as well as the right, from Quaker peace activism to the role black churches play in mobilizing the African-American vote. Last April [2004], in a review of *The Jesus Factor*, a PBS program about the role of Bush's evangelical faith in his presidency, Salon critic Charles Taylor stated with startlingly unselfconscious candor that the scary thing about [George W.] Bush was not that he injected his faith into politics, but that he was using it to promote a right-wing rather than left-wing agenda—in Taylor's words, to serve narrow constituencies rather than a "legitimate civil interest" such as raising taxes on the rich.

Given the liberal intelligentsia's high tolerance for the use of traditional religion in progressive causes, it's not surprising that hardly anyone questions the political influence of Earth-worshipping environmentalism, which novelist Michael Crichton has called "the religion of choice for urban atheists." This environmentalist "spirituality" pervades Gore's 1992 book *Earth in the Balance*.

There is some truth to the conservative claim that liberal hand wringing about the intrusion of faith into politics often smacks of politically correct bigotry. The war in Iraq and the War on Terror were widely portrayed as a part of Bush's religiously inspired crusade against "evildoers." Many Bush critics, from British political commentator Rupert Cornwell in *The Independent* to Jim Wallis of the liberal evangelical magazine *Sojourners*, have even decried his use of the word evil, in reference to people who crash airplanes into buildings, as evidence of religious fanaticism.

Moratorium on God

Yet the faith-based presidency is genuinely troubling. This is not only because of the public policies justified by invoking God's name. No less important is the symbolic message that one must be religious in order to be a part of the body politic —in order, perhaps, to be a "real" American. It's a message that goes hand in hand with a good deal of secularist bashing and particularly atheist bashing: In some of the Republican attacks on Democratic financier George Soros, atheist was used as a term of opprobrium.

The public's views on this subject are more complex than the champions of religion in the public square often make them out to be. For instance, a recent *Time* poll found likely voters evenly divided on the question of whether the president should allow his personal faith to be his guide in making political decisions. The vast majority of Americans consider themselves religious, but about a third do not consider religion very important in their lives and attend religious services once a month or less. That's a pretty large segment of the population to reduce to the status of political pariahs.

The idea that politicians should keep their religious faith private may seem outrageously intolerant. But is it not equally outrageous that, on today's political scene, a secularist figure cannot express his views honestly without committing career suicide? Unlikely though it is to happen, a moratorium on God talk might level the playing field.

"*By declaring an all-out war against the 'evil principle' of democracy, [terrorist] Zarqawi and his followers are thus swimming against the current of Muslim public opinion and the spirit of the times.*"

Islam and Democracy Are Compatible

Fawaz A. Gerges

In this viewpoint, originally published in 2005 when Iraq had its first free election, Fawaz A. Gerges argues that Muslims who claim that Islam and democracy are incompatible are in the minority. He contends that diatribes against democracy by terrorists do not resonate with most Muslims. Young Muslims do not want their rights violated or to live in fear because of dissenting views, Gerges asserts. Muslim scholars believe that democracy is compatible with the tenets outlined in the Koran, the Islamic holy book, according to Gerges. Gerges is a professor of Middle East studies and international affairs at Sarah Lawrence College and the author of *The Jihadists: Unholy Warriors*.

As you read, consider the following questions:

1. As stated by Gerges, how have mainstream Islamists reacted to the kidnapping and beheading of civilians by terrorists in Iraq?
2. With what negative experience with the West do Muslims worldwide associate Western liberal democracy, according to the author?

Fawaz A. Gerges, "Zarqawi and the D-Word; Is Democracy Un-Islamic?" *The Washington Post*, January 30, 2005. Copyright © 2005 by the Washington Post Book World Service/Washington Post Writers Group. Reproduced by permission of the author.

If President [George W.] Bush wanted to conjure up someone from central casting to act as a foil to his inauguration call for worldwide freedom, he couldn't ask for a villain more fitting than the terrorist leader Abu Musab Zarqawi, who, on the eve of Iraqi elections, denounced democracy as an "evil principle."

In a widely disseminated Internet audiotape, Zarqawi didn't merely say that he opposed the mechanics or timing of the U.S.-run elections being held today[1] in Iraq to choose a 275-member assembly and transitional government. And he didn't say he thought Iraqis should wait and vote after U.S. occupation forces depart. No, Zarqawi said that he opposes any elections under any circumstances.

In doing so, he sets up a clash with more at stake than the outcome of today's voting. In the audiotape, which surfaced last Sunday [January 23, 2005], Zarqawi, the most feared and wanted militant in Iraq, declared a "fierce war" against all those "apostates" who take part in the elections. He called candidates running in the elections "demi-idols" and the people who plan to vote for them "infidels." And he railed against democracy because he said it supplants the rule of God with that of a popular majority. This wicked system, he said disapprovingly, is based on "freedom of religion and belief" and "freedom of speech" and on "separation of religion and politics." Democracy, he added, is "heresy itself."

"Is Democracy Un-Islamic?"

The questions Zarqawi raises go way beyond the elections in Iraq to the whole issue of modernization of the Arab world. Is democracy un-Islamic? Is there a fundamental clash between the principles of representative government and the principles of Islam?

Increasingly, Muslims themselves are saying no. A small but influential group of Islamic intellectuals is saying that Muslims should see democracy as compatible with Islam. Islamic political parties and movements across North Africa and the Middle East are deciding with greater frequency to take part in elections whenever possible. In the Palestinian

1. Elections were held in Iraq at the time this article appeared.

Authority balloting, the radical Islamic Resistance Movement, known as Hamas, has entered candidates in races for local offices. In Egypt, Islamic political activists are urging President Hosni Mubarak to retire and permit free elections. And in Iraq, Grand Ayatollah Ali Sistani, the revered Shiite cleric, issued an edict saying participation in the balloting today was a "religious duty."

That explains, in part, the recent increase in violence in Iraq. Zarqawi and other foes of democracy cannot rely on public sentiment to keep people away from the polls. Instead they must turn to fear, instilled by suicide bombings and brutal attacks. Hardly a day has gone by without insurgents threatening to "wash the streets of Baghdad with the voters' blood." The intimidation campaign is relentless. "Oh people, be careful. Be careful not to be near the centers of blasphemy and vice, the polling centers. . . . Don't blame us but blame yourselves" if you are harmed, a Web statement issued in the group's name last week said.

Zarqawi Echoes bin Laden

Zarqawi's diatribe against democracy echoed the views of Osama bin Laden who, in an audiotape broadcast in December, endorsed Zarqawi as his deputy in Iraq and called for a boycott of the Iraqi elections. "In the balance of Islam, this constitution is heresy, and therefore everyone who participates in this election will be considered infidels," he said. Bin Laden lashed out at fellow Muslims who support the electoral process, admonishing listeners to "beware of henchmen [such as Sistani and other clerics] who speak in the name of Islamic parties and of groups who urge people to participate in this blatant apostasy." For bin Laden, Zarqawi and other militants in Iraq, the goal is not just to drive Americans out of the war-torn country but also to impose their own reactionary theocratic model on Iraq. In their eyes, democracy is the antithesis of puritan Islam.

Although foreign militants such as Zarqawi number fewer than 1,000, according to Gen. George W. Casey Jr., the commander of U.S. forces in Iraq, they appear to have made informal but effective alliances with homegrown radical Sunni rebels with whom they share an intrinsic loathing of democracy. In December, three militant Iraqi groups, including the guerrilla group Ansar al-Sunna, issued a statement warning that people taking part in the "dirty farce" risked attack. "Democracy is a Greek word meaning the rule of the people, which means that the people do what they see fit," they said. "This concept is considered apostasy and defies the belief in one God—Muslims' doctrine." Ansar al-Sunna had earlier posted a manifesto on its Web site saying that democracy amounted to making idols of human beings.

The bad news is that these insurgents are gaining momentum and could frighten Iraqis away from the polls today. A very low Sunni Arab turnout could call into question the legitimacy of the elections and the new government. And antidemocratic forces could make further inroads into the Sunni Arab community, especially if Iraqi Sunnis feel excluded and disenfranchised after the vote. A senior moderate Sunni official who is running for office was asked what would happen if the Shiites won a landslide victory. "We will all join the armed resistance," he retorted. The longer turmoil continues, the more likely it is that Iraq could replace Afghanistan as the main recruiting ground for jihadi causes and become a magnet for international terrorism.

Majority Are Not Anti-Democratic

The good news is that the anti-democratic rhetoric by Zarqawi and bin Laden crystallizes the political choices facing Muslims worldwide. The jihadis' antidemocratic stance is unpalatable to the overwhelming majority of Muslims. Mainstream clerics and Islamists have condemned the kidnapping and beheading of civilians and other abuses. After the U.S.-led assault on the insurgent stronghold in Fallujah in November, Zarqawi lashed out at senior Muslim scholars and clerics for their silence and tepid backing. "You have let us down in the darkest circumstances and handed us over to the enemy," he reportedly said on an audiotape.

Although leading Sunni Iraqi clerics and scholars have supported resistance against the U.S. occupiers and an election boycott, they insist that they do not oppose democracy and say that they intend to get involved in politics after the vote. In defiance of the jihadis' threats, the Muslim Scholars

Association (which has links to insurgents, says it represents 3,000 mosques and is the most influential Sunni group to back an election boycott) called on Sunni Arabs to help write a constitution and join the political process. If the jihadis' antidemocratic message does not resonate with conservative Muslim scholars, it won't fly with most Iraqis.

A Terrorist Leader Vilifies Democracy

In the audiotape [released in January 2005], a speaker identifying himself as Abu Musab al-Zarqawi—the leader of Iraq's al-Qaida [terrorist group] affiliate—called candidates running in the elections "demi-idols" and said those who vote for them "are infidels."

"We have declared a fierce war on this evil principle of democracy and those who follow this wrong ideology," the speaker said. "Anyone who tries to help set up this system is part of it"—a clear warning to both candidates and those who choose to vote.

The speaker warned Iraqis to be careful of "the enemy's plan to implement so-called democracy in your country."

Sameer N. Yacoup, Associated Press, Sunday, January 23, 2005.

Outside Iraq, the attitudes of mainstream Islamists, such as the powerful Muslim Brotherhood, toward political participation and representation have come a long way in the last three decades.

Rethinking Democracy and Islam

For reasons of strategy as well as belief, some Muslim intellectuals are rethinking the relationship between Islam and democracy and are Islamizing, not rejecting, democracy and modernity. Terminology matters. You cannot sell Western liberal democracy to Muslims worldwide because Muslims associate it with Western colonialism and power. But some Muslims are trying to give democracy an Islamic dress while embracing essentials such as elections, human rights and the rule of law.

Sheik Rachid Ghannouchi, leader of the Tunisian Renaissance Islamic party, has written that democracy can shield the Islamic community from autocrats, rather than serve as a sword for fighting secularists. Though a vehement critic of

Israel (he once said that Israeli civilians were legitimate targets), he has become a voice of moderation in Islamic politics. He argues that rule of law, elections and citizens' ultimate control over the executive are consistent with the Islamic concepts of shura (consultation), ba'ya (oath of allegiance) and ijma (consensus). And if elected Islamic regimes fail to live up to their promises, Ghannouchi insists that citizens have the right to oust their leaders. While he says that Islamic and secular democracies cannot be the same, he rejects the notion that "Islamic democracy" must mean perpetual rule by the Islamists.

The Islamic democratic movement is a work in progress. Unfortunately, pro-Western Arab and Muslim dictators, not Islamic activists, keep the gates of power locked and block any real democratic opening. In most of the Middle East, they are the jihadis' unintentional allies in the fight against the empowerment of ordinary men and women.

Zarqawi, bin Laden and other jihadis miscalculate monstrously if they think their anti-democratic diatribes will resonate with ordinary Muslims. Indigenous calls for democratic reforms are being heard in almost every corner of the Muslim world, including Iran, Egypt, Algeria, Saudi Arabia, Syria and Pakistan. Muslim human rights groups and civil society leaders are challenging the autocratic status quo and risking arrest and persecution. The democratic genie is already out of the bottle.

Swimming Against the Current

Young Muslims, in particular, long to be in charge of their lives, and they are a huge constituency. They are fed up with autocrats and false prophets alike. Young Muslims do not want their human rights violated or to live in perpetual fear because of their dissenting views. They want their dignity back and long to be proud of their countries, which are falling further behind the rest of humanity.

By declaring an all-out war against the "evil principle" of democracy, Zarqawi and his followers are thus swimming against the current of Muslim public opinion and the spirit of the times. Few Muslims will buy into their nihilistic and apocalyptic nightmare.

> *"Muslims should not be duped into believing that they can have their cake and eat it.
> . . . Islam is incompatible with democracy."*

Islam and Democracy Are Incompatible

Amir Taheri

In the following viewpoint Iranian journalist Amir Taheri argues that Islam is incompatible with democracy. He says that the notion of political equality, central to democracy, cannot be reconciled with Islam. In Islam, claims Taheri, the non-believer cannot be the equal of the believer. In the minds of Muslims, according to Taheri, democracy subverts the authority of God and subjects believers to the rule of the ignorant. Taheri has authored nine books, contributed articles to newspapers throughout the United States, Europe, and the Middle East, and is a commentator for CNN.

As you read, consider the following questions:

1. The author says democracy means the rule of the people, but in Islam, to whom does power belong?
2. According to Taheri, Islam divides human activities up into how many categories, ranging from permitted to the sinful?
3. To what does the author attribute the fact that almost all Muslim states today are failures?

Amir Taheri, "Islam and Democracy: The Impossible Union," *The Sunday Times*, May 23, 2004. Copyright © 2004 by the Times Newspapers Ltd. Reproduced by permission.

In recent weeks [in 2004] there has been soul-searching, in the Islamic world and among the wider Muslim diaspora about whether Islam is compatible with democracy. This sparked a debate hosted by Intelligence2, a forum I took part in last week. As an Iranian now living in a liberal democracy, I would like to explain why Islam and democracy are essentially incompatible.

To understand a civilisation it is important to comprehend the language that shapes it. There was no word in any of the Muslim languages for democracy until the 1890s. Even then the Greek word entered Muslim vocabulary with little change: democrasi in Persian, dimokraytiyah in Arabic, demokratio in Turkish.

Democracy is based on one fundamental principle: equality.

The Greek word isos is used in more than 200 compound nouns, including isoteos (equality), isologia (equal or free speech) and isonomia (equal treatment).

No Equality in Islam

Again we find no equivalent in any of the Muslim languages. The words we have such as barabari in Persian and sawiyah in Arabic mean juxtaposition or separation.

Nor do we have a word for politics. The word siassah, now used as a synonym for politics, initially meant whipping stray camels into line. (Sa'es al-kheil is a person who brings back lost camels to the caravan.) The closest translation may be: regimentation.

Nor is there mention of such words as government and the state in the Koran. Early Muslims translated numerous ancient Greek texts, but never those related to political matters.

The idea of equality is unacceptable to Islam. For the non-believer cannot be the equal of the believer. Even among the believers only those who subscribe to the three Abrahamic religions: Judaism, Christianity and Islam, known as the "people of the book" (Ahl el-Kitab), are regarded as fully human. Here, too, there is a hierarchy, with Muslims at the top.

Non-Muslims can, and have often been, treated with decency, but never as equals. There is a hierarchy even for animals and plants. Seven animals and seven plants will assuredly go to heaven while seven others of each will end up in hell.

Power Is God's

Democracy means the rule of the demos, the common people, or what is now known as popular or national sovereignty. In Islam, however, power belongs only to God: al-hukm l'illah. The man who exercises that power on Earth is known as Khalifat al-Allah, the regent of God. Even then the Khalifah, or Caliph, cannot act as legislator. The law has already been spelt out and fixed forever by God.

The only task that remains is its discovery, interpretation and application. That, of course, allows for a substantial space in which different styles of rule could develop.

But the bottom line is that no Islamic government can be democratic in the sense of allowing the common people equal shares in legislation. Islam divides human activities into five categories from the permitted to the sinful, leaving little room for human interpretation, let alone ethical innovations.

To say that Islam is incompatible with democracy should not be seen as a disparagement of Islam. On the contrary, many Muslims would see it as a compliment because they believe that their idea of rule by God is superior to that of rule by men, which is democracy.

The great Persian poet [Jalaluddin] Rumi pleads thus:

Oh, God, do not leave our affairs to us
For, if You do, woe is us.

Islamic tradition holds that God has always intervened in the affairs of men, notably by dispatching 124,000 prophets or emissaries to inform the mortals of his wishes and warnings.

Many Islamist thinkers regard democracy with horror.

Democracy Forgets God

The late Ayatollah [Ruhollah] Khomeini[1] called democracy "a form of prostitution", because he who gets the most votes wins the power that belongs only to God.

Sayyid Qutb, the Egyptian who has emerged as the ideo-

---

1. Khomeini led the 1979 revolution that brought Islamic rule to Iran.

logical mentor of Salafists (fundamentalists who want to return to the idyllic Islamic state of their forebears) spent a year in the United States in the 1950s. He found "a nation that has forgotten God and been forsaken by Him; an arrogant nation that wants to rule itself".

Last year Yussuf al-Ayyeri, one of the leading theoreticians of today's Islamist movement, published a book in which he warned that the real danger to Islam did not come from American tanks and helicopter gunships in Iraq but from the idea of democracy and the government of the people.

Maudoodi, another of the Islamist theoreticians now fashionable, dreamt of a political system in which humans would act as automatons in accordance with rules set by God.

He said that God has arranged man's biological functions in such a way that their operation is beyond human control. For our non-biological functions, notably our politics, God has also set rules that we have to discover and apply once and for all so that our societies can be on autopilot, so to speak.

Democracy Causes Ills

The late Saudi theologian, Sheikh Muhammad bin Ibrahim al-Jubair, a man I respected though seldom agreed with, believed that the root cause of contemporary ills was the spread of democracy.

"Only one ambition is worthy of Islam," he liked to say, "to save the world from the curse of democracy: to teach men that they cannot rule themselves on the basis of man-made laws. Mankind has strayed from the path of God, we must return to that path or face certain annihilation."

Those who claim that Islam is compatible with democracy should know that they are not flattering Muslims.

In the past 14 centuries Muslims have, on occasions, succeeded in creating successful societies without democracy. And there is no guarantee that democracy never produces disastrous results (after all, Hitler was democratically elected).

The fact that almost all Muslim states today can be rated as failures or, at least, underachievers, is not because they are Islamic but because they are ruled by corrupt and despotic elites that, even when they proclaim an Islamist ideology, are, in fact secular dictators.

Democracy Is Rule by the Ignorant

[The ancient Greek philosopher] Socrates ridiculed the myth of democracy by pointing out that men always call on experts to deal with specific tasks, but when it comes to the more important matters concerning the community, they allow every Tom, Dick and Harry an equal say.

In response his contemporary, Protagoras, one of the original defenders of democracy, argued: "People in the cities, especially in Athens, listen only to experts in matters of expertise, but when they meet for consultation on the political art, ie of the general question of government, everybody participates."

Electoral Democracies 2003

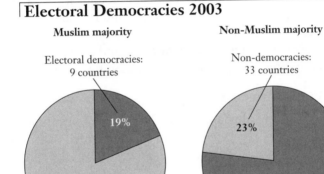

Muslim majority

Electoral democracies:
9 countries

19%

81%

Non-democracies:
38 countries

Non-Muslim majority

Non-democracies:
33 countries

23%

77%

Electoral democracies:
112 countries

www.csmonitor.com.

Traditional Islamic political thought is closer to Socrates than to Protagoras. The common folk, al-awwam, are regarded as "animals". The interpretation of the divine law is reserved only for the experts.

Political power, like many other domains including philosophy, is reserved for the "khawas" who, in some Sufi traditions, are even exempt from the rituals of the faith.

The "common folk", however, must do as they are told either by the text and tradition or by fatwas (edicts) issued by the experts. Khomeini used the word "mustazafeen" (the feeble ones) to describe the general population.

Islam is about certainty (iqan) while democracy is about doubt. Islam cannot allow people to do as they please, even in the privacy of their bedrooms, because God is always present, all-hearing and all-seeing.

There is consultation in Islam: wa shawerhum fil amr (and consult them in matters). But, here, consultation is about specifics only, never about the overall design of society.

In democracy there is a constitution that can be amended or changed. The Koran, however, is the immutable word of God, beyond amendment or change.

Islam Is an Issue in the West

This debate is not an easy one to have, because Islam has become an issue of political controversy in the West.

On the one hand we have Islamophobia, a particular affliction of those who blame Islam for all the ills of our world. Some Muslims regard any criticism of Islam as Islamophobia.

On the other hand we have Islamoflattery, which claims that everything good under the sun came from Islam. (According to a recent BBC documentary on Islam, even cinema was invented in the 9th century by a Muslim lens maker in Baghdad, named Abu-Hufus!)

This is often practised by a new generation of the Turques de profession, westerners who are prepared to apply the rules of critical analysis to everything under the sun except Islam.

They think they are doing Islam a favour. They are not.

Islamic Nations Are Not Democracies

Depriving Islam of critical scrutiny is bad for Islam and Muslims, and ultimately dangerous for the whole world. There are 57 nations in the Organisation of the Islamic Conference (OIC). Not one is yet a democracy.

We should not allow the everything-is-equal-to-everything-else fashion of postmodernist multiculturalism and political correctness to prevent us from acknowledging differences and even incompatibilities in the name of a soggy consensus.

If we are all the same, how can we have a dialogue of civilisations?

Muslims should not be duped into believing that they can have their cake and eat it. Muslims can build successful societies provided they treat Islam as a matter of personal, private belief and not as a political ideology that seeks to monopolise the public space shared by the whole of humanity and dictate every aspect of individual and community life. Islam is incompatible with democracy.

Periodical Bibliography

The following articles have been selected to supplement the diverse views presented in this chapter.

Rob Boston	"The Forgotten Founder: Long Before Madison and Jefferson Gave Us Church-State Separation, Roger Williams Fought for Soul Liberty'," *Church & State*, April 1, 2003.
Dale Butland	"Merger of Religion, Politics, Poses Risk to Our Democracy," *Cincinnati Post*, February 23, 2004.
Steven L. Carter	"Liberalism's Religion Problem," *First Things: A Monthly Journal of Religion and Public Life*, March 1, 2002.
Nader Hashemi	"Islam, Democracy and Alexis de Tocqueville," *Queens Quarterly*, March 22, 2003.
M.A. Muqtedar Khan	"The Rise of Political Christianity," *National Catholic Reporter*, December 10, 2004.
Jane Lampman	"Easing into Islamic Democracy," *Christian Science Monitor*, May 29, 2003.
Bill Moyers	"Democracy in the Balance," *Sojourners*, August, 2004.
Richard John Neuhaus	"Religion and Democracy: A Necessary Tension," *First Things: A Monthly Journal of Religion and Public Life*, June 1, 2004.
Robert O'Neil	"Church-State Separation: A View from the Pew," *Free Inquiry*, April 1, 2004.
George Cardinal Pell	"Is There Only Secular Democracy?" *Acton Institute for the Study of Religion and Liberty*, October 13, 2004. www.acton.org.
James M. Sloat	"The Subtle Significance of Sincere Belief: Tocqueville's Account of Religious Belief and Democratic Stability," *Journal of Church and State*, September 22, 2000.
Lee Teng-hui	"Confucian Democracy," *Harvard International Review*, September 22, 1999.
Helen Thomas	"Let's Keep Religion Out of Presidential Race," TheBostonChannel.com, June 23, 2004. www.thebostonchannel.com.
Jim Wallis	"God's Politics, a Better Choice: Why Can't Personal Ethics and Social Justice—Together— Become a Real Political Choice?" *Sojouners*, February 1, 2005.

Jennifer Wheary   "Who Owns America's Moral Values?" *Denver Post*, January 2, 2005.

Ellen Willis   "Freedom from Religion: What's at Stake in Faith-Based Politics," *Nation*, February 19, 2001.

Scott Yenor   "Natural Religion and Human Perfectibility: Tocqueville's Account of Religion in Modern Democracy," *Perspectives on Political Science*, January 1, 2004.

CHAPTER 3

Should U.S. Elections Be Reformed?

Chapter Preface

Democracy was founded 2,500 years ago in Athens, Greece. Although America also calls itself a democracy, historian Barry Strauss has observed that ancient Athenians would not consider America a democracy at all. The difference between ancient Greece and modern America is that Greece was a direct democracy and America is what founding father Thomas Jefferson called "this new principle of representative democracy." In representative democracy, voters elect representatives who rule the country. In the direct democracy of Athens, voters ruled directly in legislative bodies. America has some direct democracy. For example, voters in many states are asked to approve constitutional amendments through direct voting. However, Americans primarily participate indirectly in democracy by electing representatives. The indirect nature of America's democracy has been the source of many of the nation's most thorny political issues, primarily centered on the question of whether those elected actually serve the people's best interests.

Given the problematic nature of representative democracy, why did America's founders not choose direct democracy? Many analysts believe that the founders mistrusted direct democracy. According to Strauss, "None of the Founders was willing to entrust government power to poor people. . . . Left to their own devices, ordinary people were too ignorant and excitable to offer good government." Founding father James Madison believed voters needed protection from "the tyranny of their own passions." Also, the founders, having just freed America from the tyranny of England, also mistrusted any political system that would grant a person, group, institution, or state too much power.

Another important argument the founders made against direct democracy was that it is only workable on a small scale. John Adams said, "In a large society, inhabiting an extensive country, it is impossible that the whole should assemble to make laws. The first necessary step, then, is to delegate power." A related reason against direct democracy was that the serious deliberation required to adopt wise laws was thought not possible without convening face to face. James

Madison observed, "In a [direct] democracy, the people meet and exercise the government in person. A [direct] democracy must consequently, be confined to a small Spot."

Despite the reasoned arguments made by America's founders in support of representative democracy, such a political system generates problems, some of which were envisioned by the ancient Greeks. According to Strauss, the ancient Athenians believed that without direct democracy, government would "be run not only by an elite but in the interests of an elite." Some would say that the Athenians were right, that American democracy has become an oligarchy in which elected representatives run government for the benefit of the special interest groups that fund their campaigns. Indeed, many critics claim that the men and women elected by the voters do not have the voters' best interests at heart when making political decisions.

Authors in this chapter debate the merits of some of the institutions and practices central to America's representative democracy, including the electoral college, the role of campaign finance in elections, and the fairness of prohibiting felons from voting. The nature of America's democratic system ensures that such debates will continue well into the future.

"The choice of the chief executive must be the people's, and it should rest with none other than them."

The Electoral College Should Be Abolished

Bradford Plumer

Bradford Plumer argues in the following viewpoint that the electoral college, in which voters do not directly vote for a candidate but instead vote for a slate of electors who elect the president, allows electors to deny the will of the people and "vote for whomever they please." Plumer argues that this approach to electing presidents defies the will of the people. Plumer contends that the reasons given for keeping the electoral college are outdated or illogical. Plumer is an editorial fellow at MotherJones.com

As you read, consider the following questions:

1. According to a poll quoted by the author, how many voters would prefer direct elections instead of the electoral college?
2. If there is a tie in electoral votes, causing the election to be decided in the House of Representatives, how many votes are allowed each state's delegation?
3. How would direct elections affect the likelihood of recounts, according to the author?

What have Richard Nixon, Jimmy Carter, Bob Dole, the U.S. Chamber of Commerce, and the AFL-CIO all, in their time, agreed on? Answer: Abolishing the electoral college! They're not alone; according to a Gallup poll in 2000, taken shortly after Al Gore—thanks to the quirks of the electoral college—won the popular vote but lost the presidency, over 60 percent of voters would prefer a direct election to the kind we have now. This year [2004] voters can expect another close election in which the popular vote winner could again lose the presidency [the contest was not close enough for this to be an issue]. And yet, the electoral college still has its defenders. What gives?

As George C. Edwards III, a professor of political science at Texas A&M university, reminds us in his new book, *Why the Electoral College Is Bad for America*, "The choice of the chief executive must be the people's, and it should rest with none other than them." Fans of the electoral college usually admit that the current system doesn't quite satisfy this principle. Instead, Edwards notes, they change the subject and tick off all the "advantages" of the electoral college. But even the best-laid defenses of the old system fall apart under close scrutiny. The electoral college has to go.

Electing Electors

Under the electoral college system, voters vote not for the president, but for a slate of electors, who in turn elect the president. If you lived in Texas, for instance, and wanted to vote for Kerry, you'd vote for a slate of 34 Democratic electors pledged to Kerry. On the off-chance that those electors won the statewide election, they would go to Congress and Kerry would get 34 electoral votes. Who are the electors? They can be anyone not holding public office. Who picks the electors in the first place? It depends on the state. Sometimes state conventions, sometimes the state party's central committee, sometimes the presidential candidates themselves. Can voters control whom their electors vote for? Not always. Do voters sometimes get confused about the electors and vote for the wrong candidate? Sometimes.

The single best argument *against* the electoral college is what we might call the disaster factor. The American people should consider themselves lucky that the 2000 fiasco was the biggest election crisis in a century; the system allows for much worse. Consider that state legislatures are technically responsible for picking electors, and that those electors could always defy the will of the people. Back in 1960, segregationists in the Louisiana legislature nearly succeeded in replacing the Democratic electors with new electors who would oppose John F. Kennedy. (So that a popular vote for Kennedy would not have actually gone to Kennedy.) In the same vein, "faithless" electors have occasionally refused to vote for their party's candidate and cast a deciding vote for whomever they please. This year, one Republican elector in West Virginia has already pledged not to vote for Bush; imagine if more did the same. Oh, and what if a state sends *two* slates of electors to Congress? It happened in Hawaii in 1960. Luckily, Vice President Richard Nixon, who was president over the Senate, validated only his opponent's electors, but he made sure to do so "without establishing a precedent." What if it happened again?

Perhaps most worrying is the prospect of a tie in the electoral vote. In that case, the election would be thrown to the House of Representatives, where state delegations vote on the president. (The Senate would choose the vice-president.) Because each state casts only one vote, the single representative from Wyoming, representing 500,000 voters, would have as much say as the 55 representatives from California, who represent 35 million voters. Given that many voters vote one party for president and another for Congress, the House's selection can hardly be expected to reflect the will of the people. And if an electoral tie seems unlikely, consider this: In 1968, a shift of just 41,971 votes would have deadlocked the election; In 1976, a tie would have occurred if a mere 5,559 voters in Ohio and 3,687 voters in Hawaii had voted the other way. The election is only a few swing voters away from catastrophe.

At the most basic level, the electoral college is unfair to voters. Because of the winner-take-all system in each state, candidates don't spend time in states they know they have no chance of winning, focusing only on the tight races in the "swing" states. During the 2000 campaign, seventeen states didn't see the candidates at all, including Rhode Island and South Carolina, and voters in 25 of the largest media markets didn't get to see a single campaign ad. If anyone has a good argument for putting the fate of the presidency in the hands of a few swing voters in Ohio, they have yet to make it.

Arguments for and Against

So much for the charges against the electoral college. The arguments in favor of the electoral college are a bit more intricate. Here's a quick list of the favorite defenses—and the counterarguments that undo them.

The founding fathers wanted it that way!

Advocates of the electoral college often appeal to the wisdom of the Founding Fathers—after all, they set up the system, presumably they had something just and wise in mind, right? Wrong. History shows that the framers whipped up the electoral college system in a hurry, with little discussion and less debate. Whatever wisdom the Founding Fathers had, they sure didn't use it to design presidential elections. At the time, most of the framers were weary after a summer's worth of bickering, and figured that George Washington would be president no matter what, so it wasn't a pressing issue.

Most of the original arguments in favor of an electoral college system are no longer valid. The electoral college was partially a concession to slaveholders in the South, who wanted electoral clout without letting their slaves actually vote. (Under the electoral college, slaves counted towards a state's electoral vote total.) The framers also thought that ordinary people wouldn't have enough information to elect a president, which is not necessarily a concern today.

It protects state interests!

States don't really have coherent "interests," so it's hard to figure out exactly what this means. (Is there something, for instance, that all New Yorkers want purely by virtue of being New Yorkers?) Under the current system, presidents rarely campaign on local issues anyways—when George Edwards analyzed campaign speeches from 1996 and 2000, he found only a handful that even mentioned local issues. And that's as it should be. We have plenty of Congressmen and Senators who cater to local concerns. The president should take a broader view of the national interest, not beholden to any one state or locale.

It's consistent with federalism!

All history students recall that the Great Compromise of 1787 created the House, which gives power to big populous states, and the Senate, which favors small states. The compromise was just that, a *compromise* meant to keep delegates happy and the Constitution Convention in motion. Nevertheless, the idea that small states need protection has somehow become legitimated over the years, and is used to support the electoral college—which gives small states disproportionate power in electing a president. But what, pray tell, do small states need protection *from*? It's not as if big states are all ganging up on Wyoming. The fiercest rivalries have always been between regions, like the South and North in the 1800s, or between big states, like California and Texas today. Furthermore, most small states are ignored in presidential campaigns, so it's not clear that the current system is protecting anything.

More Erroneous Assertions

It protects minorities!

Some college buffs have argued that, since ethnic minorities are concentrated in politically competitive states, the electoral college forces candidates to pay more attention to minorities. This sounds great, but it's wholly untrue. Most African-Americans, for instance, are concentrated in the South, which has rarely been a "swing" region. Hispanic voters, meanwhile, largely reside in California, Texas, and New York, all uncompetitive states. It's true that Cubans in Florida have benefited wonderfully from the electoral college, but they represent an extremely narrow interest group. All other minority voters have *less* incentive to vote. It's no surprise that the electoral college has often enabled presidential candidates to ignore minorities in various states—in the 19th century, for instance, voting rights were poorly enforced in non-competitive states.

It makes presidential races more cohesive!

In an August [2004] column for *Newsweek*, George Will argued that the electoral college somehow makes presidential elections more cohesive. Again, fine in principle, untrue in practice. Will first suggests that the system forces candidates to win a broad swath of states, rather than just focusing on the most populous regions. But even if that happened, how is that worse than candidates focusing on a few random swing states? Or take Will's claim that the electoral college system prevents "factions" from "uniting their votes across state lines." What? Factions already exist—white male voters vote Republican, African-Americans vote Democrat; evangelicals vote Republican, atheists vote Democrat. If our polarized country is a concern, it has little to do with the electoral college.

Electoral College Based on Outdated Assumptions

The electoral college was devised not only to reflect American federalism—the fact that the United States was a union of separately governed states—but also to give disproportionate power to small states: They could choose electors equal in number to their delegation in the House of Representatives, plus an added elector for each of their two senators. As a result, Delaware, which now has one-tenth of New Jersey's population, has one-fifth as many electors. This arrangement created the possibility that a presidential candidate could win the popular vote nationally but lose in the electoral college which is exactly what happened [in 2000].

John B. Judis, *The American Prospect*, January 1, 2001.

Finally, Will argues that the electoral college strengthens or legitimizes the winner. For example, Woodrow Wilson won only 41.8 percent of the popular vote, but his 81.9 percent electoral vote victory "produced a strong presidency." This suggests that voters are fools and that the electoral vote total somehow obscures the popular vote total. (If a candidate gets 45 percent of the popular vote, voters aren't going to think he got more than that just because he got 81 percent of the electoral vote total. And even if they do, do we really want a system whose aim is to mislead voters about election results?) Furthermore, there's no real correlation between a strong electoral vote showing and a strong presidency. George H.W. Bush received 426 electoral votes, while Harry Truman received only 303 in 1948 and George W. Bush a mere 271 in 2000. Yet the latter two were undeniably "stronger" presidents in their dealings with Congress. There's also no evidence that an electoral landslide creates a "mandate" for change. The landslides in 1984 and 1972 didn't give Reagan or Nixon a mandate for much of anything—indeed, those two presidents got relatively little done in their second terms.

Direct elections would be a disaster

Even after all the pro-college arguments have come unraveled, college advocates often insist on digging in their heels and saying that a direct election would be even worse. They're still wrong. Here are the two main arguments leveled against direct elections:

Direct Elections

1. The recounts would kill us!

It's true, a nationwide recount would be more nightmarish than, say, tallying up all the hanging chads in Florida.[1] At the same time, we'd be *less* likely to see recounts in a direct election, since the odds that the popular election would be within a slim enough margin of error is smaller than the odds that a "swing" state like Florida would need a recount. Under a direct election, since it usually takes many more votes to sway a race (as opposed to a mere 500 in Florida), there is less incentive for voter fraud, and less reason for candidates to think a recount will change the election. But set aside these arguments for a second and ask: why do so many people fear the recount? If it's such a bad idea to *make sure* that every vote is accurately tallied, then why do we even have elections in the first place?

2. Third parties would run amok!

The ultimate argument against the electoral college is that it would encourage the rise of third parties. It might. But remember, third parties already play a role in our current system, and have helped swing the election at least four times in the last century—in 1912, 1968, 1992 and 2000.

1. In the 2001 presidential election there was controversy over how to count punch-card votes when the machine had left a "chad" (had not fully punched the hole).

Meanwhile, almost every other office in the country is filled by direct election, and third parties play an extremely small role in those races. There are just too many social and legal obstacles blocking the rise of third parties. Because the Democratic and Republican parties tend to be sprawling coalitions rather than tightly-knit homogenous groups, voters have every incentive to work "within the system". Likewise, in a direct election, the two parties would be more likely to rally their partisans and promote voter turnout, which would in turn *strengthen* the two-party system. And if all else fails, most states have laws limiting third party ballot access anyways. Abolishing the electoral college won't change that.

It's official: The electoral college is unfair, outdated, and irrational. The best arguments in favor of it are mostly assertions without much basis in reality. And the arguments against direct elections are spurious at best. It's hard to say this, but [former senator] Bob Dole was right: Abolish the electoral college!

> "*The genius of the present [Electoral College] system . . . is the genius of a popular democracy organized on the federal principle.*"

The Electoral College Should Not Be Abolished

Tara Ross

In this viewpoint Tara Ross argues that because the Founders created a republic, not a direct democracy, they intended to check the tyranny of the majority by having state electors rather than individual voters elect the president. The electoral college, she argues, protects voters in small states, who would be virtually ignored by candidates otherwise. The electoral college also provides stability to elections, she contends, because the electoral vote margin of victory is normally much larger than the popular vote margin. Ross is the author of *Enlightened Democracy: The Case for the Electoral College*.

As you read, consider the following questions:

1. Winning 50.1 percent of the votes is as effective as winning 100 percent in terms of electoral votes. How does this fact affect presidential campaigning, in the author's view?
2. According to Ross, how does the electoral college affect moderation and compromise?
3. In the twenty-six elections held between 1900 and 2000, how many have been decided by an electoral vote margin of two hundred or more, as stated by Ross?

C ontrary to modern perceptions, the founding generation did not intend to create a direct democracy. To the contrary, the Founders deliberately created a republic—or, arguably, a republican democracy—that would incorporate a spirit of compromise and deliberation into decision-making. Such a form of government, the Founders believed, would allow them to achieve two potentially conflicting objectives: avoiding the "tyranny of the majority" inherent in pure democratic systems, while allowing the "sense of the people" to be reflected in the new American government. Moreover, a republican government, organized on federalist principles, would allow the delegates to achieve the most difficult of their tasks: enabling large and small sovereign states to live peacefully alongside each other.

The authors of the Constitution had studied the history of many failed democratic systems, and they strove to create a different form of government. Indeed, James Madison, delegate from Virginia, argued that unfettered majorities such as those found in pure democracies tend toward tyranny. Madison stated it this way:

> [In a pure democracy], [a] common passion or interest will, in almost every case, be felt by a majority of the whole; a communication and concert results from the form of government itself; and there is nothing to check the inducements to sacrifice the weaker party or an obnoxious individual. Hence it is that such democracies have ever been spectacles of turbulence and contention; have ever been found incompatible with personal security or the rights of property; and have in general been as short in their lives as they have been violent in their deaths.

Alexander Hamilton agreed that "[t]he ancient democracies, in which the people themselves deliberated, never possessed one feature of good government. Their very character was tyranny; their figure, deformity." Other early Americans concurred. John Adams, who signed the Declaration of Independence and later became President, declared, "[D]emocracy never lasts long. It soon wastes, exhausts, and murders itself. There never was a democracy yet that did not commit suicide." Another signatory to the Declaration of Independence, Benjamin Rush, stated, "A simple democracy . . . is one of the greatest of evils.

Despite these strong statements against democracy, the Founders were also strong advocates for self-government, and they often spoke of the need to allow the will of the people to operate in the new government that they were crafting. "Notwithstanding the oppressions & injustice experienced among us from democracy," Virginia delegate George Mason declared "the genius of the people must be consulted." James Madison agreed, speaking of the "honorable determination which animates every votary of freedom to rest all our political experiments on the capacity of mankind for self-government."

Republican Government

The delegates, then, faced a dilemma. Their fierce opposition to simple democracy ran headlong into their determination to allow the people to govern themselves—and they knew that voters in small states would need to be free to govern themselves, just as would citizens in large states. The Founders reconciled these seemingly conflicting needs by creating a republican government, organized on federalist principles, in which minorities would be given many opportunities to make themselves heard.

The Electoral College was considered to fit perfectly within this republican, federalist government that had been created. The system would allow majorities to rule, but only while they were reasonable, broad-based, and not tyrannical. The election process was seen as a clever solution to the seemingly unsolvable problem facing the Convention—finding a fair method of selecting the Executive for a nation composed of both large and small states that have ceded some, but not all, of their sovereignty to a central government. "'[T]he genius of the present [Electoral College] system,'" a 1970 Senate report concluded, "'is the genius of a popular democracy organized on the federal principle.'"

Much has changed since 1787. The Founders could not have foreseen the rapid technological advancements, massive federal bureaucracy, and increasingly populist attitudes that characterize American life today. Could it be that the Electoral College, although once an ingenious solution to many 18th century problems, has today become merely an anachronism—and a potentially dangerous one at that?

The Electoral College undoubtedly operates in a different society from the one that existed in 1787. Yet the Electoral College has shown an amazing ability to adapt to modern-day America. It may sometimes operate differently than expected, but it still serves the political goals it was intended to serve. In truth, its operation in modern times may be even more valuable.

Wasted Votes?

Critics of the Electoral College allege that the country's presidential election process does more to trample the rights of individuals than to protect federalism. In this context, they often cite the "winner-take-all" method employed by most states, claiming that it causes the votes of some individuals to be "wasted." As this argument goes, a Texan who voted for Al Gore in the 2000 election wasted his vote because George W. Bush was awarded the state's entire slate of electors under the winner-take-all method. Gore did not win so much as one electoral vote from Texas, despite winning nearly 2.5 million of that state's popular votes during the election. In a direct popular election, critics note, these votes would not have been "wasted"—they could have instead been included in the final national tally for Gore.

Such arguments, however, are a bit disingenuous. These

votes were not wasted. They were simply cast on the losing side of a popular vote within the state. If the 2000 election had been conducted based on nationwide popular vote totals only, would people claim that any vote for George W. Bush was "wasted" because Al Gore won the popular vote? Of course not. The votes for Bush were cast in an effort to win. In the event of a loss, they would simply have been votes for the losing candidate—just as in any other election (such as an election for Governor or Senator).

The primary effect of America's federalist presidential election process is to protect the freedom of individuals—particularly those in small states and sparsely populated areas. Perhaps the best method of demonstrating the benefits of federalism is to expose the evils suffered without it.

National Campaigning

As the system stands today, presidential candidates have no incentive to poll large margins in any one state. Winning 50.1 percent of the votes in a state is as effective as winning 100 percent of the votes. Presidential candidates therefore tour the nation, campaigning in all states and seeking to build a national coalition that will enable them to win a majority of states' electoral votes. Direct popular elections, by contrast, would present different incentives. Suddenly, winning 100 percent of the votes is better than winning 50.1 percent of the votes. In fact, it may be easier to rack up votes in a friendly state than to gain 50.1 percent of votes in each of two states of similar size, although the payoff would be essentially the same.

The result? Democrats would almost certainly spend most of their time in the large population centers in California and New York. Republicans would campaign in the South and Midwest. Large cities would be focused on almost exclusively as the candidates seek to turn out as many votes as possible in "their" region of the country. Small states, rural areas, and sparsely populated regions would find themselves with little to no voice in presidential selection. In this scenario, a handful of states (or heavily populated cities) win, while the remaining states and less-populated areas suffer significantly.

Many critics dispute this description of the two types of

elections. They contend that the current system does not encourage presidential candidates to tour the nation, but instead encourages a focus on mid-sized "swing" states. "Safe" states and small states, they allege, do not receive nearly as much attention on this national tour.

There is an element of truth in this observation. Yet to the degree that safe states do not receive a proportionate amount of attention during campaigns, the logical conclusion is that those states, by and large, must already feel that one of the two presidential candidates represents their interests fairly well. When a candidate ceases to adequately understand and represent one of "his" state's interests, the discontent in that state is usually expressed pretty quickly.

Consider the situation in West Virginia in recent decades. Democrats considered West Virginia a safe state for years; thus, the state probably saw less post-nomination campaign activity from 1960–2000 than it might have otherwise. However, in 2000, the Bush campaign recognized an opportunity to gain a foothold in the state due to concern about the impact of Gore's environmental policies on the coal-mining industry and his support for gun control. Bush took advantage of this discontent, and he spent more than $2 million communicating his message to West Virginia's voters. When election results were tallied, Bush became the first Republican since 1928 to win an open race for the presidency in West Virginia. In 2004, West Virginia is no longer considered a safe state for Democrats.

Protects Small States

A second argument made by critics is similarly flawed. Although the winner-take-all system causes large states (especially large swing states) to elicit more attention than small states, these critics erroneously compare the amount of campaigning in small versus large states under the current system. They should instead compare the treatment of small states under the current system against the treatment they would receive under a new one. Today, small states undoubtedly receive less attention than large states (unless, of course, the large state is considered a safe state). However, a direct vote system would magnify, not improve, this problem because it would encourage a focus on highly populated areas. Small states would likely never receive as much attention as their larger neighbors. The goal is not to eliminate this disparity, but to minimize its severity. Under the Electoral College system, the states are as evenly represented as possible, given that they are not all the same size.

One interesting twist to the arguments raised by Electoral College critics focuses on the reality that even if *small states* benefit from the Electoral College, they do so at the expense of the *individuals* who reside in small states. This complaint can be confusing because it sounds like the opposite of another complaint—that the two vote add-on for small states (giving all a "guaranteed minimum" of three electoral votes) creates a bias in their favor. The two extra electoral votes given to all states, regardless of population, do create an advantage for those states. As a statistical matter, however, the advantage plays in favor of the *state as a whole*, rather than the *individual voter.* By contrast, the mathematical advantage granted by the winner-take-all system plays in favor of individual voters in the larger states. These voters have a statistically higher probability of materially affecting the outcome of the election.

As a purely statistical matter, perhaps this assessment is accurate. However, the odds of any one voter providing the "tipping point" in an election are still exceedingly small. Further, any individual disadvantage for those who reside in small states is outweighed by the larger advantage given to the state as a whole.

In sum, the nation conducts democratic, popular election —but they are conducted at the state level, rather than the national level. Professor Charles R. Kesler of Claremont McKenna College explains: "In truth, the issue is democracy with federalism (the Electoral College) versus democracy without federalism (a national popular vote). Either is democratic. Only the Electoral College preserves federalism, moderates ideological differences, and promotes national consensus in our choice of a chief executive."

National Base Required

Presidential candidates must build a national base among the states before they can be elected. They cannot target any one interest group or regional minority. Instead, they must achieve a consensus among enough groups, spread out over many states, to create a broad-based following among the voters. Any other course of action will prevent a candidate from gaining the strong base needed to win the election. The necessity of building such a national base has led to moderation and a strong two-party system in American politics. . . .

Victory Margins Magnified

Historically, most elections have not been close in the Electoral College, even when the popular vote is close. The Electoral College system, when combined with the winner-take-all rule, tends to magnify the margin of victory, giving the victor a certain and demonstrable election outcome. The magnification of the electoral vote can work to solidify the country behind the new President by bestowing an aura of legitimacy.

Margin of Victory in the Electoral College: 1804 to Present

Electoral Vote Margin	1804–1896 elections	1900–2000 elections	Total
200 or more	3	17	20
101–20	8	5	13
51–100	8	2	10
1–50	4	2	6
Decided in contingent election	1	0	1
TOTAL	24	26	50

Data from Congressional Quarterly, *Presidential Elections: 1789–1996* (1997) and U.S. National Archives and Records Administration.

The election of 1960 was one such close election. John Kennedy won only 49.7 percent of the popular vote, compared to Nixon's 49.5 percent. However, Kennedy won 56.4 percent of the electoral vote, compared to Nixon's 40.8 percent. Eight years later, this magnification effect worked in favor of Nixon. Although he won the popular vote by less than one percent, he won 55.9 percent of the electoral vote to Hubert Humphrey's 35.5 percent. This magnification effect increases dramatically as popular vote totals spread apart. For instance, in 1952, the winning candidate won 55.1 percent of the popular vote, but a much larger 83.2 percent of the Electoral College vote. In 1956, the difference was 57.4 percent (popular vote) to 86.1 percent (electoral vote). In 1964, it was 61.1 percent (popular vote) to 90.3 percent (electoral vote).

Presidential elections since 1804 have generally seen wide margins of victory in the Electoral College. These margins have gotten wider, on average, through the years as the winner-take-all rule has been adopted by more states and the two-party system has solidified. Since 1804, only two elections—those in 1876 and 2000—were won by fewer than 20 electoral votes. Six elections were won by fewer than 50 electoral votes: Four of these were held in the 1800s. Of the 26 elections held between 1900 and 2000, 17 Presidents have been elected after winning the electoral vote by a margin of 200 votes or more.

These consistently wide margins of victory in the Electoral College have come about despite the fact that the margin between the top two candidates in the popular vote was less than 10 percent in 14 of the 26 elections held since 1900. This margin exceeded 20 percent only five times since 1900.

A direct popular election, by contrast, would not grant certainty nearly as often. Close popular votes, such as those discussed above, could easily result in demands for recounts on a national scale. America rarely has close electoral votes. It does, however, have close popular votes fairly consistently. Do Americans really want a presidential election system that could result in hotly contested recounts nearly every election?

"Corporations are not in the business of giving something for nothing. Money buys action and influence."

Campaign Finance Laws Should Be Reformed

Noreena Hertz

In the following viewpoint Noreena Hertz argues that the huge amounts of money spent on political campaigns means that elections cannot be free and fair. She argues that big business is the only interest group that can afford to bankroll political campaigns, which means that their interests are put ahead of the public interest. Politicians have been tainted by allegations of favoritism toward corporate backers, she maintains, making it appear that they are for sale, thereby undermining citizens' faith in democracy. Hertz is associate director of the Centre for International Business at the University of Cambridge. Her book, *The Silent Takeover*, which has been translated into eight languages, is the source of this viewpoint.

As you read, consider the following questions:

1. According to Hertz, on average how much campaign money must each senator raise during each day of his or her six-year term to fund an average senatorial campaign?
2. From 1987 through 1996, how much did tobacco companies contribute to Congress and the two major parties, as stated by the author?
3. How much did America's largest five hundred corporations give to Democrats and Republicans from 1987 through 1996, according to Hertz?

Noreena Hertz, *The Silent Takeover: Global Capitalism and the Death of Democracy.* New York: The Free Press, 2001. Copyright © 2001 by Noreena Hertz. Reproduced by permission of The Free Press, an imprint of Simon & Schuster Macmillan, and the author.

[W]hy do political parties in a democracy need to raise so much money in the first place? Because in the absence of clear ideological distinctions, parties can most effectively differentiate themselves in terms of marketing strategy and spending. Not only do politicians now defer to big business, politics itself emulates corporate tactics. Door-to-door canvassing, leafleting, and local meetings were the politics of yesteryear: low-cost, low-tech, and labor-intensive. The politics of today is expensive, businesslike, and capital-intensive, and relies to a greater extent than ever before on mass communication via the media and advertising. Newspaper and magazine advertisements; terrestrial, cable, and satellite television commercials (where these are permitted); and Internet spots are today's methods of reaching what we will see to be an ever more elusive electorate. Twenty-second ads are countered by twenty-second ads, and no party or politician can afford to be outspent by rivals.

Expensive Media Circus

In the United States a phalanx of political consultants leads the way, seeking to engage voters with new and bolder ploys from direct mail campaigns to hard-hitting TV ads, with TV stations netting around $600 million in the 2000 election. Remember the [George W.] Bush ad campaign in which the word "rats" appeared subliminally in a broadcast targeting Democratic health care proposals? In Britain, by the 1990s advertising and public relations were already fully established as a part of political campaigning. [Author Martin Harrop has observed that] "[w]hen the Conservative Party hired [ad company] Saatchi and Saatchi in 1978, it was headline news. By the end of the 1980s it would have been just as big news if a major party had chosen not to use professional marketing expertise in an election." Political media advisers, advertisers, and image makers have become minor celebrities, their names probably as widely recognized as those of many cabinet ministers or congressmen.

The cost of the new media circus is truly astronomical, especially in the United States. In the run-up to the 2000 presidential elections, the candidates seeking nomination raised and spent over $1 billion—the most in U.S. history—following the $651 million spent on campaigning in the 1996 congressional elections; and the 1998 House and Senate midterm elections, in which more than $1 billion was spent, seven times the total for the 1978 election, and almost double the 1992 amount. On average an individual Senate campaign now costs $6 million, meaning that each senator, as well as each defeated candidate, must raise an average of $2,750 every single day of his or her six-year term to pay for it. Access to elected political office in the United States is now almost exclusively the privilege of the seriously rich. In his first four months of campaigning for the 2000 election, George W. Bush raised $37 million, more than either Bill Clinton or Bob Dole raised during the entire campaign in 1996. Jon Corzine, the former chairman of Goldman Sachs, spent $36 million of his own money to win a Senate seat; Michael Bloomberg $50 million of his to become mayor of New York; and defeated candidate Michael Huffington laid out as much as $30 million when he stood for the Senate in California. It is not possible to raise that kind of money from raffle tickets or barbecues. How can elections be free and fair when only the bankrolled can participate?

These developments are not unique to the USA. Although the figures are smaller, similar trends can be observed elsewhere. In an increasingly global political environment in which politicians are less able to deliver on actual policy and content, they need more money to capture their audience's attention. The 1997 general election was the most expensive British campaign to date, with the Labour Party spending just under £27 million and the Conservatives £28.5 million, double the amount spent in the 1992 election. Although under new legislation enacted under [Tony] Blair, party campaign spending in an election year will now be capped at £20 million. In Taiwan the world's wealthiest political party, the Kuomintang (KMT), paid voters between fifteen and forty-five dollars to turn up at campaign rallies for the 2000 presidential election. In Russia, the Our Home Is Russia party hired the German supermodel Claudia Schiffer and rap artist MC Hammer to provide support in the 1993 parliamentary elections.

This level of campaign spending is inherently problematic. The escalating costs of running campaigns and supporting political parties can no longer be met by membership contributions, union funds (where they are given), or personal donations. Even in countries that provide some degree of direct state funding to political parties, the funds provided by the state are nowhere near enough for today's political extravaganzas. [Author Paul Heywood has observed that] "[t]he democratic political process costs money—in ever increasing amounts." So who do politicians turn to, to meet the shortfall? As Grandma would say, the private sector, of course.

All over the world from Moscow to Paris, from Washington to London, corporations and businesspeople are bankrolling politicians and political parties. Parties and candidates are given support; money is contributed to campaigns; political rhetoric is publicly endorsed; unwritten IOUs are registered.

Such funding comes from a small elite. In the United States, for example, [according to author Charles Lewis of the Center for Public Integrity] "only one quarter of 1 percent of the population gave two hundred dollars or more to congressional candidates or the political parties in the 1995–'96 election cycle and 96 percent of the American people [didn't] give a dime to any politician or party at the federal level." America's largest five hundred corporations, on the other hand, gave over $260 million to the Democrats and Republicans from 1987 through 1996.

Buying Influence

Of course, corporations are not in the business of giving something for nothing. Money buys action and influence. In exchange for amounts of money that are often quite small from their point of view, they expect a significant return. As Supreme Court Justice David Souter has said, "There is certainly an appearance . . . that large contributors are simply going to get a better service, whatever that service may be, from a politician than the average contributor, let alone no contributor." So when Charles Keating, the boss of an American thrift company, Lincoln Savings and Loan, that later defaulted and cost the American government and taxpayer hundreds of billions of dollars, was asked whether the $1.3 million he had donated to five senators' campaigns had influenced their behavior, he replied, "I certainly hope so." Mr. Keating could afford to be frank, because his contributions were above board and entirely legal.

Despite their legality, such donations undoubtedly create an undesirable opaqueness. It is always difficult to prove a link between corporate funding and policy changes that favor a donor company, but the string of unproven connections and unlikely coincidences that link financial contributions and favorable policy changes is becoming just too long to explain away. . . .

In the USA, where the problem is probably more widespread and of a greater magnitude than elsewhere in the developed Western world, we see countless examples of probable cause and effect. For example, the Center for Public Integrity draws attention to the 1994 Fair Trade in Financial Services Act, which had been lobbied for by NationsBank, for whom the legislation would mean savings of $50 million a year. [According to the Center for Public Integrity] "[t]wo weeks later, the cash-strapped Democratic National Committee (DNC) received a $3.5 million line of credit from the NationsBank at a favorable interest rate."

Tainted Politicians

There are many similar examples. In 1993 Al Gore broke his public pledge to support the creation of a publicly funded information superhighway, advocating private funding in its place. Within a couple of days, the DNC received $132,000 from major telecommunications companies. Other generous donors to the DNC were given seats on a diplomatic trade mission with the former commerce secretary, the late Ron Brown, where companies subsequently garnered international contracts worth billions.

Many prominent American politicians have been tainted by allegations that they have given preferential access to their corporate backers. In 1992, for example, House Democratic Leader Richard Gephardt of Missouri persuaded President [Bill] Clinton not to tax beer as a means of financing his proposed health care plan; since 1988 Gephardt has received over $300,000 in campaign contributions from the Anheuser-Busch Company, the country's largest brewer. Even [Senators] Bill Bradley and John McCain, who both stood on campaign finance reform tickets in the presidential primaries, seem tainted. Mr. Bradley, while senator for New Jersey, apparently supported forty-five special bills aimed at offering tariff reductions and export aid to companies producing highly toxic chemicals. During that same period, chemical firms were among the biggest donors to his election fund. Senator McCain was accused of intervening with the Federal Communications Commission on behalf of a major contributor to his campaign, Paxson Communications, and of trying to stop the expansion of a national park in Nevada—a move which would have benefited the property development company Del Webb, his seventh biggest sponsor.

The protection given to tobacco interests in the United States, although recently undermined by product liability litigation in some states, further illustrates the influence that money can buy. . . .

The list of links between campaign donations and votes in

Congress is almost endless. Jennifer Shecter of the Center for Responsive Politics collates campaign contributions and the resultant votes by legislators who receive them. She notes: "The ten House and ten Senate members who received the largest contributions from the American sugar industry all voted to preserve a sugar quota that keeps prices high for consumers. Similar matchups are made for the timber industry, the B-2 bomber, the gambling industry, and even drunk-driving legislation, among others." In fact it has been argued that the very reason why Microsoft's monopoly was ever addressed by the U.S. government was that Bill Gates did not join the campaign and lobbying bandwagon soon enough—Microsoft had, as recently as 1995, no Washington office. A strategy that was subsequently reversed, with Microsoft over the three years of investigations and litigation nearly tripling its campaign contributions and more than doubling its lobbying expenditures. And it was to good effect: the Justice Department decided to no longer seek a breakup of the computer giant—a decision very much in line with the pledge made by [presidential candidate George W.] Bush in his attemps to woo Silicon Valley prior to the 2000 elections when he promised to support "innovation over litigation every time."

Public Finance Would Remove Corruption

When politicians elected on someone's bill, the group or groups who financed that election own the politician for the duration of the politicians' term.

Greg Mathis, *New Pittsburgh Courier*, November 3, 2004.

George W is, of course, the king of the "revolving doors" school of politics, having recruited key officials to his administration direct from the nation's boardrooms. [Vice President] Dick Cheney was headhunted from the oil services company Haliburton. Karl Rove, Bush's chief political strategist, had been chief political strategist for Philip Morris from 1991 to 1996; Mitchell Daniels, the head of the White House Office of Management and Budget, is a former vice president of Eli Lilly; and the treasury secretary, Paul O'Neill, came from the giant aluminum manufacturer Alcoa.

Politics for Sale

And since taking up office Bush has passed a series of laws that appear to favor big business. He has scrapped a raft of work safety measures which had been negotiated between the federal government and the unions for much of the previous decade. He proposed a bankruptcy bill, long demanded by the banks and credit card companies who sponsored Bush and his party to the tune of over $25 million, whose effect will be to strip Americans who have declared themselves bankrupt from some of the legal protection they have from their financial creditors. And he has passed a number of measures intent on protecting the interests of the energy companies that bankrolled his campaign. In addition to withdrawing from the Kyoto Protocol on global warming, the president reversed several executive directives passed in the final days of the Clinton administration, which aimed to protect 58 million acres of federal land by restricting logging and road building; he reneged on his own campaign pledge to regulate carbon dioxide emissions from power plants; he discussed the opening up of the vast and virgin Arctic wilderness in Alaska for prospecting and drilling; and he reversed Clinton decrees on clean-air standards for buses and big trucks. He also allowed Enron executives (good judgment here—not) to vet candidates for the commission regulating the U.S. energy markets, filling the vacant Republican seats on the commission with commissioners who had the backing of Enron and other power companies. The interests of the American people were suborned to those of the major U.S. energy giants that bankrolled him: $25.4 million was all it cost.

Politics has been on sale even in issues with potential national security implications. In 1997, for example, President Clinton overrode the objections of the Justice Department, and permitted an American company, Loral Space and Communications, to export technology to China that would allow it to improve its nuclear missile capabilities, granting a waiver to sanctions that had been imposed after the 1989 massacre of hundreds of prodemocracy protesters in Tiananmen Square. Bernard Schwartz, chairman of Loral, was the largest personal donor to the Democrats that year. President Clinton, of course, denied any quid pro quo. "The decisions we made were made because we thought they were in the interests of the American people," he later said. Which American people was that, exactly?

And it has been argued that the Bush administration initially blocked Secret Service investigations into Islamic terrorism because of the influence of powerful oil corporations, many of whom had stumped up wads of money for the Bush campaign. John O'Neill, former head of the FBI's counterterrorism office in New York, who later became head of security at the World Trade Center and was killed in the September 11 attacks, left his FBI job complaining that his investigations into Al Qaeda had been obstructed, stating that "the main obstacles to investigating Islamic terrorism were U.S. corporate oil interests and the role played by Saudi Arabia.". . .

Money Makes Politicians Listen

The connection between corporate donations and policy decisions is, of course, not always clear-cut. While the American gun lobby is a large contributor to political campaigns—in 2000 it hosted the biggest fund-raiser ever in American politics, raising $21.3 million for the Republicans in one night—it also has genuine mass support. And many politicians support local industries not only because they donate money to campaigns, but because jobs, and therefore votes, are tied up in these industries. [Author Lars-Erik Nelson argues that] "[d]airy state representatives like Senator Pat Leahy, a Vermont Democrat, will vote to protect dairy interests whether or not they receive cash contributions from dairymen."

Whether or not definite causal links can be found, what is clear is that by making money available to politicians, or bankrolling the armies of lobbyists that now fill the corridors of power, corporations and businesspeople are at least ensuring that politicians listen to their demands and consider what they want. After all, why would business bother if they didn't think donations were likely to serve their interests generally, if not specifically through bills or policy decisions? But by permitting a system that allows such transfers to take place, politicians are essentially admitting their inability to control "corporate creep"—their willingness to rate the interests of certain groups higher than those of others.

"*Low levels of campaign spending are not likely to increase public trust, involvement, or attention, but they will tend to diminish public knowledge.*"

Campaign Finance Laws Should Not Be Reformed

John J. Coleman

In this viewpoint John J. Coleman argues that high levels of campaign spending do not breed public cynicism or distrust. In fact, high spending levels, he asserts, improve democracy by increasing the knowledge that voters have about candidates. His research also finds that the benefits resulting from campaign spending are broadly dispersed among voters with varying incomes and education levels. John J. Coleman is a professor of political science at the University of Wisconsin, Madison, and author of *Party Decline in America: Policy, Politics, and the Fiscal State.*

As you read, consider the following questions:

1. In research cited by the author, what was the correlation between campaign spending and voters' trust in the federal government "to do what is right"?
2. According to the author's research on twenty measures of voter knowledge of candidates' ideologies, how many of those measures were boosted by campaign spending?
3. How do increases in campaign spending affect the knowledge that socioeconomically disadvantaged groups have about the ideology of candidates, according to Coleman?

John J. Coleman, "The Benefits of Campaign Spending," *Cato Institute Briefing Papers*, no. 84, September 4, 2003, pp. 2–8. Copyright © 2003 by the Cato Institute. All rights reserved. Reproduced by permission.

The complaints about campaign spending are well-known. One frequent assertion is that high levels of spending alienate and disillusion the public. Does an individual's direct experience with campaign spending affect his or her attitudes? Do large amounts of spending in their own districts turn off and disillusion potential voters? Campaign spending does not have the dire consequences for trust, efficacy, and involvement that were alleged by critics of campaign spending.

In a study of the 1994 and 1996 U.S. House elections, my coauthor and I examined whether the level of spending in the campaigns affected the public's trust in government and the electoral process. In other words, are citizens living in congressional districts where campaign spending is high likely to be more cynical about politics and elections than citizens living in districts where spending is low? Merging the best available national election public opinion data (the National Election Studies, collected by the Interuniversity Consortium for Political and Social Research at the University of Michigan) with campaign spending data collected by the Federal Election Commission, we performed a statistical analysis to determine whether campaign spending was linked to the level of public trust. The study controlled for more than a dozen other factors that might influence public trust; that way, we could be certain that we were isolating the effects of campaign spending from the effects of other possible factors.

The results indicated that campaign spending does not contribute to public cynicism. When respondents were asked how often they trusted the federal government to do what is right, their answers were unaffected by the level of candidate spending. The same result held when survey respondents were asked whether people like themselves had a say in what government does. Whether campaign spending was high or low, people were equally likely to indicate that they did have a say in what government does. Direct experience of high levels of spending does not increase citizens' cynicism about government and politics. . . .

Critics often deride campaigns as exercises in manipulation, but analysis of the effects of campaign spending suggests a more positive interpretation. Higher campaign spending produces more knowledge about candidates, whether measured by knowing the candidates' names, being able to place candidates on ideology or issue scales (the survey respondent is, for example, asked where he or she would place a candidate on a seven-point ideology scale if one end of the scale is labeled "extremely liberal" and the other "extremely conservative"), or confidence in the placement on the ideology scale. For 20 measures of knowledge, we found that there was a statistically significant relationship between spending and knowledge. On 18 of those measures, spending boosted knowledge; only on 2 did spending decrease knowledge. The effects of spending are overwhelmingly positive, and they are particularly strong for challengers. That is, both incumbent and challenger spending produce boosts in knowledge, and challenger spending is more likely to do so. Those tendencies were essentially linear, meaning that we did not see evidence that knowledge boosts would fade out at any particular spending level. The upshot is that setting a cap on spending by incumbents or challengers would likely produce a less informed, less knowledgeable electorate.

For example, we found that when challenger spending was at its mean level of about $230,000 in 1996, about 49 percent of respondents in the relevant districts could place the challenger on a seven-point ideology scale. At $500,000 of spending, the percentage rose to 66; and at $1,000,000, the percentage jumped to 85. The percentage of respondents certain that their placement was correct also jumped from 20 to 31 to 53 at these three challenger spending levels.

We found similar effects for specific issues. For example, if an incumbent spent around $210,000 in 1996, about 36 percent of the public in the district would be able to place the incumbent on an issue scale for abortion. If the incumbent spent $1,500,000, about 53 percent of the public would be able to locate the incumbent somewhere on the abortion issue scale. The same pattern holds for challengers. If a challenger spent around $210,000, about 13 percent of the public would be able to place that candidate on the abortion issue scale. At $1,500,000, however, the percentage jumps to 53, the same as for incumbents. We find similar results when looking at defense spending and government services and spending, the other issue scales available in the National Election Study.

Increased spending also affects whether respondents report likes or dislikes about the challenger and incumbent, again suggesting an information effect—as respondents learn more, they may find that there are things they do or do not like about a particular candidate, or they may find that some of the things that they thought were true about that candidate do not in fact appear to be so. That again suggests a boost in public knowledge.

Money Doesn't Misinform

One of the major concerns of critics of campaign spending is that candidates allowed to spend as much as they wish will misinform and confuse the public, perhaps even use campaign funds to create false impressions about their true stances on issues. We examined this charge directly in our study and found that it is not persuasive. By combining data on how an incumbent has voted on bills in Congress (roll-call votes) with the survey respondents' placement of the incumbent on an ideology scale, we can see how accurate people are in their placement of the incumbent. In other words, if a respondent places an incumbent toward the liberal end of the ideology scale, we can see whether the incumbent's voting record has in fact been toward that end of the scale. In our study, we produce "loose," "moderate," and "strict" measures of accuracy, with each posing a more difficult threshold before considering an individual's placement of the incumbent to be accurate.

The findings are encouraging. In 1996, the more incumbents spent, the more accurate respondents were about the incumbent's ideology according to all three of our accuracy measures. If incumbents hypothetically spent $0 in running for reelection, about 23 percent of the public would be accurate about their ideological placement (using, for this example, the measure of "moderate accuracy" in the study). This level of accuracy results from familiarity with the incumbent from news reports during his or her term, as well as other cues such as the party label. Spending of $1,000,000 would lead to 49 percent of the public being accurate; spending of $1,500,000 would produce an accuracy rate of 63 percent.

This is a strong, significant improvement in public accuracy. In 1994 incumbent spending increased accuracy according to our "moderate" measure. For the other measures, there was no statistically significant relationship: additional incumbent spending does not make respondents more accurate, but it does not "fool" the public and make respondents less accurate, either. In both years, challenger spending tended to decrease accuracy about the incumbent—the more challengers spend, the less sure the public is about what the incumbent stands for. The challenger in a competitive election wants voters to wonder how much they really know about the incumbent; campaign spending raises that question for voters. The effect of more spending, then, is a more reflective and aware electorate. As incumbent spending pushes respondents in one direction, challenger spending pushes them in another. In short, incumbent and challenger spending produces a more competitive election. Limiting spending would limit competitiveness.

Money = Speech

The First Amendment says that Congress "shall make no law . . . abridging the freedom of speech, or . . . the right of the people peaceably to assemble, and to petition the Government" (that's "political association"). The campaign finance laws [that limit campaign spending] blatantly violate these prohibitions.

Robert J. Samuelson, *Washington Post*, August 25, 2004.

These results are consistent with those of another study published in 1999. There, I examined whether incumbents could use campaign spending to distance themselves from the public image of their party or from their voting records. Could an incumbent run away from the party label and from his or her own voting record? Specifically, I investigated whether incumbents could create a more moderate image of themselves through the use of campaign spending. The results showed that incumbents could not spend their way to a more moderate image than their voting record would suggest. In fact, the more incumbents spent, the less likely respondents were to mistakenly place the incumbent in the ideological center.

Overall spending does not make individuals less knowledgeable, despite what critics imply. Instead, we see substantial evidence of spending boosting awareness, recall ability to perform campaign-related knowledge tasks, and respondent accuracy.

Knowledge Benefits Broadly Dispersed

One fear often voiced by critics of campaign spending is that such spending merely perpetuates the advantages of the already well-off. The logic is that candidates tend to cater their appeals to the relatively wealthy in society. The more money spent in campaigns, the argument goes, the larger the information gap between the well-off and the less-well-off. Moreover, some citizens will pay more attention to public affairs than will others, and candidates will target their attention to those individuals. High-attention citizens tend to have more education, higher income, and higher socioeconomic status in general. Again, the more candidates spend, the larger the gap that emerges between low-attention and high-attention citizens as candidates shower the attentive group with campaign appeals—or so the story goes. As indicated above, my research has found significant knowledge benefits from campaign spending. It would be alarming if those benefits were received disproportionately by society's most advantaged citizens, thus exacerbating the gap between social classes or groups.

The question of whether campaign spending disperses knowledge broadly across the population or to more narrowly targeted groups is tied to one of the most fundamental issues that has animated political science scholarship for decades: does a particular political practice enhance equality or foster inequality? This is simple, direct, and profoundly important to democratic theory.

My research suggests that, as with campaign spending in general, the story is a relatively positive one. In my study, I compared the effects of campaign spending for a series of group pairings, in which the first group would be considered relatively advantaged politically, economically, or socially and the second group would be considered relatively disadvantaged. The group pairs included political characteristics (for example, strong partisans vs. not strong partisans, contacted by party vs. not contacted by party, voters vs. nonvoters) and socioeconomic characteristics (for example, white vs. not white, family income in top 75 percent vs. family income in bottom 25 percent, attended at least some college vs. attended no college). I also created a cumulative measure of advantage and disadvantage that combined four group characteristics; the "cumulatively advantaged" are advantaged in at least three of these characteristics (high income, college education, voter).

I then examined several knowledge items relevant to House campaigns, such as recall of candidate names, placing candidates on ideology scales, and placing candidates on issue scales. Because much of the controversy in campaign spending research concerns the fate of challengers, I focused on the impact of challenger spending on knowledge about the challenger, comparing the impact for people in the advantaged groups with the impact for people in the disadvantaged groups.

The results show that the benefits of campaign spending are broadly dispersed across advantaged and disadvantaged groups alike. That is, as challengers spent more, members of both groups gained in knowledge. For example, with challenger spending at $225,000 in 1996, 57 percent of members of the "cumulatively advantaged" group could place the challenger on a seven-point liberal to conservative ideology scale. Forty-seven percent of non-cumulatively advantaged ("disadvantaged") individuals could do the same. If challenger spending increases to $650,000, the percentages are 78 and 69 for the two groups, respectively. With spending at $1.3 million, the percentages leap to 94 and 90, respectively. This example shows that increased spending produces real increases in the knowledge of both the relatively advantaged and the relatively disadvantaged. Moreover, the disadvantaged make real gains on the advantaged. At $225,000, the ratio between the percentage of the disadvantaged (47 percent) and the percentage of the advantaged (57 percent) able to place a challenger on the ideology scale is .82 (in other words, the ratio of 47 percent to 57 percent is .82). At $650,000, the ratio is .88. At $1.3 million, it is .96. At that level of spending, the gap in knowledge between the two socially disparate groups has nearly evaporated.

To take another example, at $225,000 of challenger spending in 1996, 18 percent of the cumulatively advantaged could place the challenger on a seven-point issue scale for government services and spending; 13 percent of the disadvantaged could do so. The ratio of the two is .72. At $650,000, the percentages increase to 35 and 26, respectively, with a ratio of .74. At $1.3 million, the percentages are 67 and 58, respectively, with a ratio of .87. Again, the more money spent, the more both groups are able to perform this task. The more the challenger spends, the closer the ratio of the percentage of people in each group that can place the challenger on the scale. And this example shows that there is clearly room for even more gains in knowledge as spending exceeds $1.3 million.

What both of these examples show is that limiting challenger spending to $225,000, or $650,000, or even $1.3 million would have a negative consequence in terms of public knowledge and that the consequence would spread acres social political and economic groups. Many other examples can be drawn from the research to make the same point: When more money is spent, relatively advantaged groups do gain the benefit of more knowledge, but, particularly critical for democratic elections, so do relatively disadvantaged groups. Increased knowledge about the candidates does not disproportionately flow to privileged sectors of society, bypassing less privileged sectors. Campaign spending has the effect (through campaign ads, contacts, and other organizational activity) of dispersing knowledge broadly across the public, to relatively disadvantaged as well as advantaged groups. The more that is spent, the more equal groups become in their knowledge levels. Low levels of spending, therefore, lock in inequality of knowledge between groups. Campaign spending, rather than strengthening and entrenching political inequality, is a democratizing force. . . .

Challengers Need to Spend

Political scientists have long thought that, terms of competitive elections, low levels of spending can be problematic. Ordinarily, of course, incumbents have the spending advantage. Congressional incumbents are often quite good at what they do. They have name recognition; they know how to use the media; they know how to work on issues that are of interest in the district; they take positions that are generally popular in the district; and they know how to get things done for the district and for individual constituents. Challengers frequently need to spend more than incumbents to overcome those nonfinancial advantages of incumbency. Challengers allowed to spend freely might well topple incumbents, especially where incumbents are weak and unpopular. When an incumbent is weak, of course, money will tend to flow into the challenger's campaign more readily. Restricting that inflow makes the job of displacing the incumbent that much more difficult.

Campaign spending has been not only a source of complaints about the reelection of incumbents; it has also become a surrogate for a wide range of problems in the political system. Despite the volume of the public debate, there has been little academic research focusing directly on the impact of campaign spending on public trust, efficacy, involvement, and knowledge. These are questions about our civic life that are broader than the issue of who wins and who loses elections. The series of studies reported in this paper is a sustained attempt to track those linkages at the national level. The findings of those studies show that campaign spending enhances the quality of democracy and leads to a vibrant political community. Spending does not diminish trust, efficacy, and involvement, contrary to critics' charges. Moreover, spending increases public knowledge about the candidates, across essentially all groups in the population, whether "advantaged" or "disadvantaged." The policy implication of these findings is that low levels of campaign spending are not likely to increase public trust, involvement, or attention, but they will tend to diminish public knowledge. Spending limits, whether explicit or implicit, mean a reduction in the level of public knowledge during campaigns. Getting more money into campaigns should, on the whole, be beneficial, and there is a range of methods—which would appeal differently to people of different ideological persuasions—by which those additional resources could enter the campaign finance system. Campaign spending benefits democracy.

> "Despite wide differences in disenfranchisement laws, one common thread ties them together: . . . a disproportionate number of nonwhite citizens have been excluded from the democratic process."

Some Felons Should Be Allowed to Vote

Steven Carbo, Ludovic Blain, Ellen Braune, and Tate Hausman

In this viewpoint Steven Carbo, Ludovic Blain, Ellen Braune, and Tate Hausman argue that felony disenfranchisement laws—which bar those convicted of certain crimes from voting—have been used to discriminate against people of color. The authors note that such laws have permanently disenfranchised 13 percent of black men. Disenfranchisement, say the authors, makes it more difficult for ex-prisoners to reintegrate into society. Carbo, Blain, and Braune are the director, associate director, and communication director respectively, of Dēmos, a non-profit public policy research and advocacy organization. Hausman is a freelance editor.

As you read, consider the following question:

1. According to the authors, what percentage of black adults and white adults are disenfranchised?
2. In the authors' view, how does the harshness of state disenfranchisement laws correlate with the number of nonwhite prisoners in that state?

Steven Carbo, Ludovic Blain, Ellen Braune, and Tate Hausman, "Democracy Denied: The Racial History and Impact of Disenfranchisement Laws in the United States," *Demos: A Network for Ideas & Action*, April 2003. Reproduced by permission.

Contrary to popular belief, felony disenfranchisement laws are not part of the criminal justice system. Instead, they are state election laws, enacted by state legislatures, governors, or hardwired into constitutions by constitutional conventions. Losing the right to vote is not in any way part of a criminal sentence—it is a "collateral consequence" dictated by state law.

In other words, ex-prisoners lose their voting rights because of the intersection of two systems—the election law system and the criminal justice system. *Both systems have been used independently, to discriminate against people of color for much of American history.* Together, they create a "perfect storm" of forces that politically weaken communities of color. Law professor David Cole points out that "together, the drug war and felony disenfranchisement have done more to turn away black voters than anything since the poll tax."

The war on drugs does indeed help to explain why the incarceration rate among blacks has superseded the rate among whites. Scholars estimate that 14 percent of illegal drug users are black, yet blacks make up 55 percent of those convicted and 74 percent of those sentenced for drug possession. According to the U.S. Sentencing Commission, 65 percent of crack cocaine users are white, but 90 percent of those prosecuted for crack crimes in federal court are black—and are subject to greater penalties than powder cocaine offenders.

Unequal application of the law is not limited to drug offenses, but stretches through every aspect of the criminal justice system. In some cities, half of young black men are under the supervision of the criminal justice system at any one time, two-thirds will be arrested by age thirty, and more are in prison than in college. The public is increasingly aware of this bias. Even conservatives such as President [George W.] Bush, Attorney General John Ashcroft, and Senator Orrin Hatch describe racial profiling as a serious problem plaguing our criminal justice system.

Harsh Disenfranchisement Laws

The other half of the "perfect storm"—the election law system—varies widely from state to state. The Department of Justice recently described state-level felony disenfranchisement rules as "a national crazy-quilt of disqualifications and restoration procedures." Some states extend full voting rights to all eligible citizens, regardless of their criminal records. Others take away voting rights forever, even in the case of a first conviction.

What makes certain states adopt such harsh laws? A new study by sociology professors Christopher Uggen and Jeff Manza and law student Angela Behrens identifies race as the central factor. After extensively studying felony disenfranchisement laws from the 1850s to today, Uggen and Manza conclude that "States with larger proportions of nonwhites in their prison populations were more likely to pass restrictive laws, even when the effects of time, region, economic competition between whites and blacks, partisan control of government, and state punitiveness (as measured by overall incarceration rates) were statistically controlled." In other words, it is no coincidence that states with more nonwhite prisoners have harsher disenfranchisement laws.

Some states ostensibly allow ex-prisoners to regain their voting rights, but throw incredibly labyrinthine procedures in their path. Alabama makes some ex-prisoners submit DNA samples to regain their rights. Other states make ex-prisoners fill out forms with details like their children's birthdays and the cause of their father's death. Still others require a 2/3 supermajority of the state legislature for a pardon. Even when ex-prisoners jump through all these legal hoops, the restoration of their rights is neither speedy nor guaranteed. In 2002, Florida's Board of Clemency estimated that they had a backlog of at least 35,000 ex-prisoners who had applied for restoration of their voting rights.

Non-Whites Most Disenfranchised

Despite wide differences in disenfranchisement laws, one common thread ties them together: In nearly all states, a disproportionate number of nonwhite citizens have been excluded from the democratic process.

- Nationally, about 7.5 percent of black adults (men and women) are disenfranchised, compared to 1.5 percent of whites.
- Some 13 percent of black men, or 1.4 million citizens,

have forever lost their right to vote.

- Black men make up 36 percent of the disenfranchised population, though they make up only 6 percent of the general population.
- Given current rates of incarceration, three in ten of the next generation of African-American men will lose the vote at some point in their lifetimes.
- In six states—Alabama, Florida, Iowa, Mississippi, Virginia, and Wyoming—at least one in four black men has already become permanently disenfranchised.
- In Florida and Alabama, 31 percent of black men are barred from voting for life.

Statistics about disenfranchised Latinos have been hard to aggregate, due to inconsistent reporting and conflicting data sources. However, a recent study by the Mexican American Legal Defense and Education Fund (MALDEF) found that in six of ten sampled states, Latinos are more likely to be disenfranchised than the overall population. The most striking disparity is in New York, where preliminary data indicates that Latinos are overwhelmingly more likely than whites to have lost the vote. Given that 16 percent of Latino men in America will enter prison in their lifetime, compared to only 4.4 percent of white men, this higher percentage of disenfranchised Latinos is not surprising.

These statistics translate directly into the loss of political power. With far fewer voters among their ranks, communities of color have less influence than their population numbers should dictate, and much less control over the policies that most affect their lives—a contradiction of the fundamental American ideal of self-governance and a major impediment to truly representative democracy.

Disenfranchisement Disempowers African Americans

Felony disenfranchisement laws date back to the earliest days of the U.S. republic, and to Europe before that. Early European disenfranchisement laws seem to have been limited to the most serious crimes, and were implemented by judges in individual cases. As American states drew up their constitutions, many of them incorporated some form of disenfranchisement laws into their statutes.

At the end of the Civil War, however, lawmakers found new uses for felony disenfranchisement laws. The newly adopted Fifteenth Amendment allowed African Americans to vote—in theory. In practice, Southern whites soon began to rewrite their state constitutions to remove African Americans from politics. Declaring proudly and explicitly their goal of white supremacy, these lawmakers used a variety of legal schemes to disempower African Americans, including literacy tests, poll taxes, grandfather clauses and all-white primaries. Most of these laws have been called out as racist and unconstitutional, and have been wiped from the books. Felony disenfranchisement laws are the notable exception.

Mississippi's 1890 constitutional convention was among the first to use felon disenfranchisement laws against African Americans. Until then, Mississippi law disenfranchised those guilty of any crime. In 1890, however, the law was narrowed to exclude only those convicted of certain offenses—crimes of which African Americans were more often convicted than whites. The Mississippi Supreme Court in 1896 enumerated these crimes, confirming that the new constitution targeted those "convicted of bribery, burglary, theft, arson, obtaining money or goods under false pretenses, perjury, forgery, embezzlement or bigamy."

Other states followed suit. Many newly disenfranchisable offenses, such as bigamy and vagrancy, were common among African Americans simply because of the dislocations of slavery and Reconstruction. Indeed, the laws were carefully designed by white men who understood how to apply criminal law in a discriminatory way: the Alabama judge who wrote that state's new disenfranchisement language had decades of experience in a predominantly African-American district, and estimated that certain misdemeanor charges could be used to disqualify two-thirds of black voters.

White Supremacy

"What is it we want to do?" asked John B. Knox, president of the Alabama convention of 1901. "Why, it is within the limits imposed by the Federal Constitution, to establish white supremacy in this State."

Categories of Felons Disenfranchised Under State Law

STATE	PRISON	PROBATION	PAROLE	EX-FELONS All*	Partial
Alabama	•	•	•	•	
Alaska	•	•	•		
Arizona	•	•	•		• (2nd felony)
Arkansas	•	•	•		
California	•		•		
Colorado	•		•		
Connecticut	•		•		
Delaware	•	•	•		• (5 years)
District of Columbia	•				
Florida	•	•	•	•	
Georgia	•	•	•		
Hawaii	•				
Idaho	•	•	•		
Illinois	•				
Indiana	•				
Iowa	•	•	•	•	
Kansas	•	•	•		
Kentucky	•	•	•	•	
Louisiana	•	•	•		
Maine					
Maryland	•	•	•		• (2nd felony, 3 years)
Massachusetts	•				
Michigan	•				
Minnesota	•	•	•		
Mississippi	•	•	•		• (certain offenses)
Missouri	•	•	•		
Montana	•				
Nebraska	•	•	•		• (2 years)
Nevada	•	•	•		• (except first-time nonviolent)
New Hampshire	•				
New Jersey	•	•	•		
New Mexico	•	•	•		
New York	•		•		
North Carolina	•	•	•		
North Dakota	•				
Ohio	•				
Oklahoma	•	•	•		
Oregon	•				
Pennsylvania	•				
Rhode Island	•	•	•		
South Carolina	•	•	•		
South Dakota	•				
Tennessee	•	•	•		• (post-1981)
Texas	•	•	•		
Utah	•				
Vermont					
Virginia	•	•	•	•	
Washington	•	•	•		• (pre-1984)
West Virginia	•	•	•		
Wisconsin	•	•	•		
Wyoming	•	•	•		• (5 years)
U.S. Total	49	31	35	6	8

* While these states disenfranchise all persons with a felony conviction and provide no automatic process for restoration of rights, several (Alabama, Kentucky, and Virginia) have adopted legislation in recent years that streamlines the restoration process.

The Sentencing Project, January 2005. www.sentencingproject.org.

The laws worked. A historian later hired by Alabama state registrars found that by January 1903, the revised constitution "had disfranchised approximately ten times as many blacks as whites," many for non-prison offenses.

Such schemes would soon be approved by the highest courts in the land. In 1896, the Mississippi Supreme Court endorsed with devastating clarity the discriminatory intent of disenfranchisement laws after Reconstruction. The Mississippi constitutional convention of 1890, wrote the court,

> . . . swept the circle of expedients to obstruct the exercise of the franchise by the negro race. By reason of its previous condition of servitude and dependence, this race had acquired or accentuated certain particularities of habit, of temperament and of character, which clearly distinguished it, as a race, from that of the whites—a patient, docile people, but careless, landless, and migratory within narrow limits, without forethought, and *its criminal members given rather to furtive offenses than to the robust crimes of the whites.* Restrained by the federal constitution from discriminating against the negro race, the convention *discriminated against its characteristics and the offenses to which its weaker members were prone. . . .* Burglary, theft, arson, and obtaining money under false pretenses were declared to be disqualifications, while robbery and murder, and other crimes in which violence was the principal ingredient, were not.

This understanding was not confined to the South. In 1898, the U.S. Supreme Court implicity endorsed Mississippi's discriminatory disenfranchisment laws in *Williams v. Mississippi,* a case that legalized all-white juries. Disenfranchisement laws were challenged again in the Supreme Court in 1974. The Court's decision in that case, *Richarson v. Ramirez,* not only upheld the laws, but also made future legal challenges harder. It took until the 1985 case *Hunter v. Underwood,* brought by two men who lost their voting rights in Alabama due to a "crime of moral turpitude"—writing bad checks—for the Court to agree that racism was an explicit purpose of felony disenfranchisement laws. But the *Hunter* decision only struck down those laws motivated by racist intent—and only the most explicit, purposeful intent. Laws with less overt racist effects, like today's felony disenfranchisement laws, have been left standing.

The racially tainted history of felony disenfranchisement

laws ought to make Americans of all ideological persuasions reconsider their value in our democracy. These policies, so closely linked to our prejudicial past, should survive only if we have an overwhelming need for them: when they alone fulfill a specific, extremely important social purpose. Felony disenfranchisement policies fail that test.

As Alec Ewald concludes in his "Punishing at the Polls" report, felony disenfranchisement runs counter to our democratic ideals. The arguments in favor of disenfranchisement are not supported by data, and in fact, disenfranchisement laws have a negative impact on the stated goals of our criminal justice system. And denying the vote to any citizen can only have negative consequences for a democratic society.

- *Disenfranchisement fails as a form of punishment*, because it does not help achieve any of the four goals penal policies pursue: incapacitation, deterrence, retribution, and rehabilitation.

- *No evidence exists that offenders would vote in a "subversive" way*, as some supporters of criminal disenfranchisement allege. Barring some citizens from the polls simply because they might vote to change our laws violates essential American principles.

- *No evidence exists that offenders are more likely than others to commit electoral fraud*, and states have numerous laws on the books that prevent and punish fraud.

- *Disenfranchisement laws have the perverse effect of encouraging recidivism*, since they make it harder for ex-prisoners to fully reintegrate into society. Restoring voting rights would speed the rehabilitation process and give ex-prisoners a meaningful stake in their communities.

- *Evidence domestically and from abroad shows that protecting voting rights for all citizens keeps a democracy healthy.* Nations as diverse as Israel, Canada, Macedonia and Sweden, and parts of the U.S. including Maine, Vermont and Puerto Rico even allow many citizens who are incarcerated to vote from their cells.

Re-Enfranchisement Movement

A growing coalition of voting rights advocates, criminal justice reformers and ex-prisoners have come together to challenge felony disenfranchisement laws. Victories have been scored in a number of states in recent years, and momentum is building to end felony disenfranchisement across the country.

At least 500,000 citizens have been re-enfranchised in the last five years due to policy changes:

- In New Mexico—where ex-felons were once disenfranchised for life—Republican Governor Gary Johnson recently signed a law to automatically restore the vote to qualified ex-felons.
- Connecticut upgraded its laws in 2001 to allow 36,000 people on probation to vote.
- In 2002, Maryland repealed a law that automatically and permanently disenfranchised people convicted of a second felony.
- In 2003, Wyoming and Alabama enfranchised some citizens after they complete their full sentence.

Riding the wave of success from these victories, an eight-member collaboration of advocacy and legal rights groups have launched Right to Vote, a national campaign to restore voting rights to ex-prisoners. Specifically targeting five states—Florida, Alabama, New York, Maryland and Texas—the coalition has launched a series of legislative, public education, voter mobilization and legal campaigns. The coalition includes the National Association for the Advancement of Colored People (NAACP), the NAACP Legal Defense Fund, Dēmos, the Brennan Center for Justice at NYU School of Law, The Sentencing Project, the Mexican American Legal Defense and Education Fund, People for the American Way, and the American Civil Liberties Union.

Significant legal challenges to felony disenfranchisement laws are working their way through the courts. In New York, a self-educated prisoner filed *Hayden v. Pataki* in 2001[1] which challenges New York's felon disenfranchisement statutes and is now being litigated by the NAACP Legal Defense Fund and two other organizations. In Florida, the Brennan Center is representing the plantiffs in *Johnson v. Bush*,[2] which at-

---

1. *Hayden* was dismissed by U.S. District Court, Southern District of New York, in 2004.   2. The Eleventh Circuit Court of Appeals ruled against the ex-felons on April 12, 2005.

tempts to re-enfranchise the 600,000 citizens who have fully finished their sentences but are still denied their voting rights. Other actions are pending in Massachusetts, Virginia and Washington.

Eventually, voting rights advocates would like to see the abolition of all criminal disenfranchisement laws—a complete and final separation of state election rules from the criminal justice system. Like past struggles against racism—the abolition of slavery, *Brown v. Board of Education*,[3] the freedom summers, the Voting Rights Act, environmental justice campaigns, and countless other fights—the battle against felony disenfranchisement laws will take a broad and determined campaign. As Dr. Martin Luther King, Jr. said, "the moral arc of the universe is long, but it bends towards justice."

---

3. *Brown* is a famous Supreme Court case ending segregation of public schools.

"The murderer . . . has expressed contempt for his fellow citizens and broken the rules of society. . . . It's fitting that society should deprive him of his role in determining the content of those rules."

Felons Should Not Be Allowed to Vote

Edward Feser

In this viewpoint Edward Feser contends that disenfranchisement laws—which bar certain criminals from voting—affects blacks more than other races because blacks commit more felonies. He argues that disenfranchisement is just because lawbreakers have shown their contempt for society by committing crimes and should have no say in voting on what the laws will be. Allowing lawbreakers to vote, says the author, devalues the right to vote. Feser teaches philosophy at Loyola Marymount University in Los Angeles.

As you read, consider the following questions:

1. According to the author, what ancient civilizations had policies of disenfranchisement?
2. In the author's opinion, what English philosopher did not consider the right to vote inalienable?
3. How does the author think losing the right to vote affects recidivism among felons released from prison?

Edward Feser, "Should Felons Vote?" *City Journal*, Spring 2005. Copyright © 2005 by the Manhattan Institute for Policy Research. Reproduced by permission.

Forty-eight states currently restrict the right of felons to vote. Most states forbid current inmates to vote, others extend such bans to parolees, and still others disenfranchise felons for life. A movement to overturn these restrictions gained swift momentum during the 2004 presidential campaign, and pending legal and legislative measures promise to keep the issue in the headlines in the months to come. It hasn't escaped notice that the felon vote would prove a windfall for the Democrats; when they do get to vote, convicts and ex-cons tend to pull the lever for the Left. Had ex-felons been able to vote in Florida in 2000—the state permanently strips all felons of voting rights—[Democrat] Al Gore almost certainly would have won the presidential election.

Murderers, rapists, and thieves might seem to be an odd constituency for a party that prides itself on its touchy-feely concern for women and victims. But desperate times call for desperate measures. After three national electoral defeats in a row, the Democrats need to enlarge their base. If that means reaching out to lock in the pedophile and home-invader vote, so be it. Even newly moderate Democrat Hillary Clinton has recently endorsed voting rights for ex-cons. This is inclusiveness with a vengeance.

The liberal advocates and Democratic politicians seeking the enfranchisement of felons deny any narrow political motivation, of course. Their interest is moral, they claim: it is just *wrong* to deny felons the vote. Their various arguments in support of this conclusion, though, fail to persuade.

Disenfranchisement Is Not Racist

The most frequently heard charge is that disenfranchising felons is racist because the felon population is disproportionately black. But the mere fact that blacks make up a lopsided percentage of the nation's prison population doesn't prove that racism is to blame. Is the mostly male population of the prisons evidence of reverse sexism? Of course not: men commit the vast majority of serious crimes—a fact no one would dispute—and that's why there are lots more of them than women behind bars. Regrettably, blacks also commit a disproportionate number of felonies, as victim surveys show. In any case, a felon either deserves his punishment or not, whatever his race. If he does, it may also be that he deserves disenfranchisement. His race, in both cases, is irrelevant.

But look where the laws preventing felons from voting arose, the advocates say: in bigoted post-Civil War legislatures, keen to keep newly emancipated blacks away from the ballot box. These laws are utterly racist in origin, like poll taxes and literacy tests. But this argument fails on two counts. First, as legal writer Roger Clegg notes, many of the same studies appealed to by felon advocates show that the policy of disenfranchising felons is as old as ancient Greece and Rome; it made its way to these shores not long after the American Revolution. By the time of the Civil War, 70 percent of the states already had such laws.

No Disproportionate Impact

Courts have been unreceptive to "disparate impact" arguments [asserting that some laws disproportionately affect a particular group], absent a showing of invidious motives. So there is no violation of the 14th Amendment guarantee of "equal protection of the laws" when all felons, black or white, are disfranchised for their decisions to break laws.

George Will, *Newsweek*, March 14, 2005.

Second, even if felon disenfranchisement *did* have a disreputable origin, it wouldn't follow that the policy is bad. To think otherwise would be to commit what logicians call the genetic fallacy. Say Abraham Lincoln drafted the Emancipation Proclamation purely for cynical political reasons, or to exact vengeance on rebellious Southern plantation owners, or just to get rid of some unneeded scratch paper. It would be silly to suggest that therefore freeing the slaves wasn't a good thing.

Felon advocates also argue that to prevent felons from voting, especially after their release from prison, unfairly punishes them twice for the same crime. On this view, the ex-con pays his debt to society by doing time and should suffer no further punishment. But this begs the question at issue: should a felon lose his vote as well as spend time behind bars? Few people would say that the drunk driver sentenced by a judge to lose his driver's license and to pay a hefty fine is punished twice. Most would agree that, given the crime, this one punishment with two components is perfectly apt. Similarly, those who support disenfranchising felons do not believe in punishing criminals twice for the same misdeed; they believe in punishing them once, with the penalty including both jail time and the loss of the vote. A punishment of incarceration without disenfranchisement, they plausibly maintain, would be too lenient.

The Right to Vote Is Not Inalienable

The claim that disenfranchising felons is wrong because the right to vote is basic and inalienable—another common argument of the advocates—is no more convincing. Obviously, the right is not basic and inalienable in any legal sense, since the laws banning murderers, thieves, and other wrongdoers from voting have stood for a long time. Nor is the right basic and inalienable in a moral sense. Even John Locke, the English philosopher generally regarded as having the greatest influence on the American founding, didn't view the franchise in that light. True, Locke believed that all human beings had certain rights by nature (such as rights to life, liberty, and property), that government existed to protect those rights, and that any legitimate government had to rest on the tacit consent of the people. But the government that the people consented to did not need to be democratic, in Locke's view—it might even be monarchical.

As long as it protected the basic rights of citizens and retained their loyalty, it remained legitimate, whether or not it allowed its citizens to vote.

Further, Locke added, under certain circumstances we can lose even the rights we do have by nature. Someone who violates another's rights to life, liberty, and property forfeits his own rights to these things; society can legitimately punish him by removing these rights. The criminal has broken the social compact and violated the trust of his fellow citizens. He cannot reasonably complain if they mete out to him a measure of the very harm that he has inflicted on them. Their doing so is a means of dissuading others from breaking the social contract.

Seen in this light, disenfranchisement seems a particularly appropriate punishment for felons. The murderer, rapist, or

166

thief has expressed contempt for his fellow citizens and broken the rules of society in the most unmistakable way. It's fitting that society should deprive him of his role in determining the content of those rules or electing the magistrate who enforces them.

A *New York Times* editorial this past February [2005] favored felon voting—no surprise there—but put forward a different rationale. The disenfranchisement of felons, the paper held, "may actually contribute to recidivism by keeping ex-offenders and their families disengaged from the civic mainstream"—a notion "clearly supported by data showing that former offenders who vote are less likely to return to jail."

The *Times*'s argument is at least more serious than those considered so far. Still, it doesn't fly. Recidivism doubtless is also less common among ex-cons who return their videos on time. That doesn't mean they should be rewarded with free rental privileges at Blockbuster. More to the point, it doesn't seem to have occurred to the *Times* that it might be misinterpreting the (alleged) causal connection between voting and keeping out of trouble. Surely it's at least plausible—in fact, quite plausible—that it is precisely the sort of person disposed to learn from his mistakes and become more conscientious who is likely to vote in the first place. That is, it isn't that voting makes someone responsible but that the responsible person will be likelier to vote.

If that's true, then a former inmate who already has what it takes to clean up his act isn't likely to relapse into a life of crime just because he can't cast a ballot. By the same logic, an ex-con hell-bent on new rapes and muggings isn't going to turn over a new leaf just because he gets to vote—even if it's to vote for a Democrat. The notion that he might is pure sentimentality. It assumes that deep inside the typical burglar or car jacker lurks a Morgan Freeman–type character, full of world-weary wisdom and latent civic virtue. A neoconservative, some say, is a liberal mugged by reality. A felon-vote advocate seems to be a liberal who has seen *The Shawshank Redemption*[1] one too many times.

1. a critically acclaimed 1994 movie set in a prison. Actor Morgan Freeman played a role in the movie.

It would be a tall order for any moral or political theory, let alone the Lockean one central to the American tradition, to make a convincing case that the disenfranchisement of felons is particularly unjust. How is depriving felons of the vote worse than stripping them of their freedom by incarcerating them? Surely the right to liberty is far more basic and fundamental than the franchise. Yet few would deny that it's legitimate to deprive serious criminals of their liberty. To do so, after all, would be to deny the possibility of criminal justice.

Disenfranchisement Is Just

Perhaps, though, some advocates of felon voting have trouble with the basic concept of criminal justice. Traditional notions of desert, punishment, and retribution aren't in fashion among those whose hearts bleed more for perpetrators than for victims. The movement to give felons the vote may be a sign that the tough-on-crime New Democrat is as passé as the [John] Kerry campaign [for president in 2004] for a whiff of the criminal-as-victim mind-set seems to surround the whole enterprise. The *Times* editorial coos over unnamed "democracies abroad" that "valu[e] the franchise so much that they take ballot boxes right to the prisons." It would have been more accurate to say that they "value the idea of individual responsibility so little that they take ballot boxes right to the prisons."

Such countries devalue the franchise by throwing it away on murderers and other criminals, whose fellow citizens' blood is still fresh on their hands. Such hands can only defile a ballot. If the right to vote is as precious as felon advocates claim to believe it is, we should expect people to uphold at least some minimum moral standards in order to keep it—such as refraining from violating their fellow voters' own inalienable rights.

Those pushing for felon voting will thus need to come up with much better arguments before they can hope to convince their fellow citizens. They ought at least to try. People might otherwise begin to suspect that the hope of gaining political advantage is the only reason they advocate reform.

Periodical Bibliography

The following articles have been selected to supplement the diverse views presented in this chapter.

Akhil Reed Amar and Vikram David Amar
"Ten Arguments in Favor of Keeping the Electoral College—Refuted!" *History News Network*, December 17, 2001. www.hnn.us.

William Benoit
"Let's Abolish the Electoral College," *Newsday*, April 19, 2004.

James D. Besser
"Is the Electoral College Good for Jews?" *JewishJournal.Com*, November 24, 2000. www.jewishjournal.com.

Glen Browder
"Guiding the Great Experiment: California's Recall and America's Democratic Destiny," *Anniston Star*, October 26, 2003.

Paul Burstein
"Is Congress Really for Sale?" *Contexts*, Summer 2003.

James R. Edwards
"Want a Real Constitutional Crisis? Scrap the Electoral College," *National Review Online*, February 20, 2002. www.nationalreview.com.

John M. de Figueiredo
"Lobbying and Information in Politics," John M. Olin Center for Law, Economics, and Business Discussion Paper No. 369, June 2002. www.law.harvard.edu.

Lee Hubbard
"Blacks and the Electoral College," *Precinct Reporter*, January 11, 2001.

James J. Lopach
"Freedom Versus Equality in Campaign Finance Reform," *Social Studies*, May 1, 2002.

Shawn Macomber
"Mob Rule: The Beauty of Direct Democracy," *American Spectator*, May 1, 2004.

James McClellan
"Q: Should the Electoral College Be Abolished in Favor of Direct Elections? Yes: The Electoral College Grossly Distorts the Principle of One Person, One Vote," *Insight on the News*, December 18, 2000.

Spencer Overton
"The Donor Class: Campaign Finance, Democracy, and Participation," *University of Pennsylvania Law Review*, 2004.

Ron Paul
"The Electoral College vs. Mob Rule," statement on the official Web site of Congressman Ron Paul. www.house.gov.

Arthur Schlesinger Jr.	"Fixing the Electoral College," *Washington Post*, December 19, 2000.
Wayne Slater	"California Recall Is Chaos to Some, Direct Democracy to Others," *Knight Ridder/Tribune Business News*, July 27, 2003.
Charles F. Williams	*"McConnell v. FEC:* Reforming Campaign Finance: Court Upholds Campaign Finance Act Despite First Amendment Dissents," *Social Education*, March 1, 2004.
Elizabeth M. Yang	"Balancing Campaign Finance Reform Against the First Amendment," *Social Education*, September 1, 2000.

CHAPTER 4

Should Democracy Be Fostered Worldwide?

Chapter Preface

Many settlers saw in colonial America an opportunity to establish an ideal society that would serve as an example to the world. John Winthrop, a leader of the Puritans who settled Massachusetts Bay in the seventeenth century, wrote in 1630, "We shall be as a City upon a hill. The eyes of all people are upon us. Soe (*sic*) that if we shall deal falsely with our God in his work we have undertaken, and so cause him to withdraw his present help from us, we shall be made a story and a byword throughout the world."

Historian G.K. Chesterton has observed, "America is the only nation in the world that is founded on a creed. That creed is set forth with dogmatic and even theological lucidity in the Declaration of Independence." The Declaration states, "We hold these truths to be self-evident, that all men are created equal, that they are endowed by their Creator with certain inalienable Rights, that among these are Life, Liberty, and the pursuit of Happiness." When the Revolutionary War was fought, it was for these principles. Founding father Thomas Jefferson wrote in 1790 that "it is indeed an animating thought that while we are securing the rights of ourselves and posterity, we are pointing out the way to struggling nations who wish, like us, to emerge from their tyrannies, also."

The notion that America has a mission to share its notions of liberty and democracy persisted in the nineteenth century. It found expression in the writings of influential editor John L. O'Sullivan. O'Sullivan wrote in "The Great Nation of Futurity" in 1839 that America

> is destined to manifest to mankind the excellence of divine principles; to establish on earth the noblest temple ever dedicated to the worship of the Most High—the Sacred and the True. . . . This is our high destiny, and in nature's eternal, inevitable decree of cause and effect we must accomplish it.

This ideal has not vanished. In recent years spreading democracy has become a stated foreign policy goal. After U.S. invasions of Afghanistan in 2001 and Iraq in 2003, America has worked to help democratize these nations. Numerous U.S. agencies provided assistance to Ukrainians during their 2004 elections, which were considered by Michael McFaul, a senior fellow at the Hoover Institute, to be "Ukraine's democratic breakthrough." In 2005 the United States also pressured Syria to withdraw from Lebanon after millions of Lebanese took to the streets in protest of Syria's occupation.

President George W. Bush expressed his agreement with the goal of spreading democracy worldwide. In *The National Security Strategy of the United States*, he states:

> People everywhere want to be able to speak freely; choose who will govern them; worship as they please; educate their children—male and female; own property; and enjoy the benefits of their labor. These values of freedom are right and true for every person, in every society—and the duty of protecting these values against their enemies is the common calling of freedom-loving people across the globe and across the ages.

Of course, not all people see the spreading of democracy as an unmitigated good. Many analysts claim that the mission to spread democracy has become a justification for global dominance. Some commentators assert that America has invaded other lands to take their resources under the pretext of spreading democracy. Despite these criticisms, the ideals expressed by Winthrop, the founders, and O'Sullivan still inform U.S. policies.

In this chapter authors debate whether spreading democracy will help prevent terrorism, whether democracy is best for all countries, and whether democracy will succeed in Iraq. The idea of democracy being the best political system has persisted in the United States since its founding and continues to shape its policies for good or ill.

"Democratic institutions and procedures . . . can help to address those underlying conditions that have fueled the recent rise of Islamist extremism."

Fostering Democracy Worldwide Will Help Prevent Terrorism

Jennifer L. Windsor

Jennifer L. Windsor argues in the following viewpoint that promotion of democracy will reduce terrorism by offering a set of values that offer an attractive alternative to extremism fueled by oppression and poverty. Democracy can provide avenues for peaceful change and productive channels for dissent and political discussion. It also promotes values such as equality, the rule of law, and human development, which all people desire, she maintains. While Democratic elections create short-term dangers such as instability, in the long run fostering democracy will bring freedom, economic prosperity, and, most important, peace to the Middle East, she asserts. Windsor is the executive director of Freedom House, a nonpartisan organization that promotes democracy and human rights.

As you read, consider the following questions:
1. Of the nine countries considered most politically repressive in the world, how many are in the Middle East, as stated by the author?
2. In Windsor's view, what accounts for the tendency of democracies to be better governed?

Jennifer L. Windsor, "Promoting Democratization Can Combat Terrorism," *The Washington Quarterly*, vol. 26, Summer 2003, pp. 43–50. Copyright © 2003 by The Center for Strategic and International Studies and the Massachusetts Institute of Technology. Reproduced by permission of The MIT Press, Cambridge, MA.

C an promoting democracy prevent renewed terrorist at-tacks against the United States? Although cynics may scoff, democratization has gained credence as a counterter-rorism strategy in the aftermath of the September 11, 2001, attacks. The underlying logic is that democratic institutions and procedures, by enabling the peaceful reconciliation of grievances and providing channels for participation in poli-cymaking, can help to address those underlying conditions that have fueled the recent rise of Islamist extremism. The source of much of the current wave of terrorist activity—the Middle East—is not coincidentally also overwhelmingly un-democratic, and most regimes in the region lack the legiti-macy and capacity to respond to the social and economic challenges that face them.

Although not without risks, and only if pursued as part of a broader strategy, democratization can help reshape the cli-mates in which terrorism thrives. More specifically, promot-ing democratization in the closed societies of the Middle East can provide a set of values and ideas that offer a power-ful alternative to the appeal of the kind of extremism that to-day has found expression in terrorist activity, often against U.S. interests.

The United States has launched a score of important post–September 11 initiatives to promote democratization in the Middle East. To be most effective, the United States must further strengthen diplomatic efforts that demonstrate to the people and the governments that human rights and democratic practices are a U.S. priority and must cohesively integrate those diplomatic messages with foreign assistance strategically directed to strengthen the forces for democratic reform within the region.

Terrorism resists simplification and easy explanation. Its causes are multifaceted and complex, and any single re-sponse to terrorism will yield only partial results. Thus, a comprehensive, dynamic policy response to combat terror-ism is necessary. This article focuses on just one important part of that policy: the promotion of democratization. Just as the thesis that poverty causes terrorism has been debunked —the masterminds of the September 11 attacks came from the wealthy and more privileged elements of society—one cannot maintain that the absence of democracy directly explains the causes of terrorism. Countless repressive countries have not generated terrorist movements; conversely, terrorist groups, including Islamic extremists, have emerged in a number of established democracies. The lack of democracy has played a role, however, in creating the conditions conducive to the recent emergence of Islamic extremist movements. As Secretary of State Colin Powell recently noted, [in 2002] "[A] shortage of economic opportunities is a ticket to despair. Combined with rigid political systems, it is a dangerous brew indeed."

Middle East Is Less Free

This article focuses on the Middle East—the epicenter of the current terrorist upsurge. In addition to being beset by economic difficulties, the Middle East is the least democratic region in the world. With the exception of Israel, none of the countries in the region demonstrates enough respect for political rights and civil liberties to be considered "Free," as classified by Freedom House in its annual survey of freedom around the world. Of the 18 countries in the region, the organization rates 13 as "Not Free"—characterized by severely limited political rights, political persecution and terror, and repression of free association and peaceful dissent—and four others as "Partly Free." Indeed, Iraq, Libya, Saudi Arabia, and Syria are four of the nine countries considered to be the most politically repressive in the world.

Whereas almost all other regions have seen unprecedented democratization in the last 30 years, the Middle East has not demonstrated any significant political progress. The region has been dominated by a range of authoritarian political systems, including military regimes, monarchies, theocracies, and one-party statist regimes. With the exception of some tactical liberalization, most regimes have resisted efforts to devolve power either horizontally, to other branches of government such as the parliament or the judiciary, or vertically, by increasing accountability to the people through free and fair elections. In his new book *The Future of Freedom*, Fareed Zakaria describes the situation as "an almost unthinkable reversal of a global pattern" in which "almost every Arab country is less free than it was forty years ago. There are few places in the world about which one can say that."

Promote Debate

The West must invest significant resources into helping to shape the minds of the next generation of Muslims. This is not simply about implanting "Western propaganda." It is about providing venues through which rational, moderate and reformist Muslims can debate freely about the future of Islam.

James J. Na, "We Can Fight Terrorism by Fostering Free Debate," *The Seattle Times*, September 28, 2004.

Throughout the Middle East, secular opposition parties lack dynamism and a broad base of political support. Civil society is weak as a result of the severe legal restrictions and coercive methods that the region's regimes use to stifle political expression. Independent media are largely nonexistent; most newspapers and articles are censored, and those that exist are seen as serving the interests of the regime or particular political parties. In such societies, severe repression drives all politics underground, placing the moderate opposition at a disadvantage and encouraging political extremism. Democratic movements and leaders by nature build support by operating openly and using traditional instruments of peaceful protest such as criticism through the media, public meetings, and mass organizations; but highly authoritarian societies prevent such activism by interdicting such activities and persecuting and imprisoning nonviolent opponents. In contrast, successful conspiracy is historically linked to authoritarian, top-down systems of control; to a cult of unity; to the suppression of diversity of opinion; and to the elaboration of obscurantist theories. Political extremists welcome brutal repression because it radicalizes activists and swells their own ranks. In this sense, the net effect of severe repression is to weaken or destroy the moderate elements within society with whom a compromise can be struck and simultaneously to empower those that seek total victory for their extremist cause.

As authoritarian repression creates an environment in which terrorist extremists can thrive, it also erodes public support for the rulers of the region. Globalization has brought an unprecedented level of commercial and cultural penetration of societies, providing populations with ready proof of their comparatively poor economic and social status. Ossified political structures are unable to deal effectively with deteriorating social and economic conditions in the Middle East, which has an annual growth rate lower than that of any region outside sub-Saharan Africa, a double-digit unemployment rate, and declining labor productivity, creating a growing crisis of legitimacy. With little possibility of improving their own lives or channeling their energies toward producing meaningful change in their own countries, the educated but unemployed youth of the Middle East have grown increasingly angry and frustrated.

The reasons behind the progression from frustration with to violence against the United States are many and complex, but certainly the distorted information flow within many Middle Eastern societies plays a role. Regimes that suffer from declining legitimacy have always tended to divert their populations' attention to evils outside their own borders. The closed nature of Middle Eastern societies contributes both to the declining legitimacy of the regimes and to the proliferation of inaccurate, polemical information manipulated for the regimes' own benefit. With populations discouraged by their lack of political and economic opportunities and hungry for a cause with which to identify and for someone to blame, as well as a media that is virulently anti-American, the Middle East is especially fertile ground for the terrorist message.

Democracy Can Help

Over the long term, the establishment of democratic political systems in the Middle East has advantages that can mitigate the great possibilities for recruitment of extremists, including the following:

- *Avenues for peaceful change of government.* Through regular, free and fair elections, the public can bring about a change of policies and can remove leaders without risking widespread political crisis.
- *Channels for dissent and political discussion.* Between elec-

tions, legislatures can debate and influence government policies. Independent media and civic society groups allow for a more accurate flow of information between the government and the populace. Local governments can provide an additional level of access and contact. As a result, democratic regimes have better governance structures that can respond to new social and economic needs, and citizens are less likely to feel powerless and unable to affect the decisions that impact their lives.

- *Rule of law.* Leaders are accountable to the law, not above it, and this reduces their incentives to engage in corrupt behavior. Legal restraints also hold the security sector in check. Citizens have access to an independent judiciary to resolve disputes and therefore do not need to resort to violence.

- *Civil society.* In democracies, civil society plays a critical role in checking political power, channeling political participation and aspirations, and encouraging the development of democratic culture. If individuals feel they have meaningful opportunities to effect change in their own countries, they are less likely to channel their energies and animosities against outside actors.

- *Free flow of information.* Democracy also encourages the free flow of information, particularly through the establishment of independent media. The population thus has access to competing sources of information. Governments are able to rely on critical feedback that can help to construct more responsive policies.

- *Strong states.* Democracies tend to be better governed and legitimized by virtue of having been chosen by their own people. They therefore tend to be strong states that do not need to rely on repression and an extensive military apparatus to control their own population and territories. As President George W. Bush noted, "[T]he events of September 11, 2001, taught us that weak states, like Afghanistan, can pose as great a danger to our national interests as strong states. . . . [W]eak states [are more] vulnerable to terrorist networks . . . within their borders."

- *Sustainable economic and social development.* The latest *Human Development Report*, produced by the United Nations Development Program, bluntly states that democracy is "essential" to human development. "[C]ountries can promote human development for all only when they have governance systems that are fully accountable to all people—and when all people can participate in the debates and decisions that shape their lives." Addressing the looming social and economic crisis, and the psychological toll that the crisis has exacted on the people of the Middle East, is critical to formulating a long-term strategy to reduce political extremism. Political freedom is an integral part of a development strategy focused on maximizing human dignity, and it encourages "individual initiative and social effectiveness," which are the driving forces behind development progress.

- *Needed values and ideals.* Democracy is grounded in certain ideals—tolerance, compromise, respect for individual rights, equality of opportunity, and equal status under law—largely absent in the region. Such values can have a powerful appeal and a revolutionary impact on how individuals view themselves and their relationship to society and government and would thus make them less vulnerable to extremist messages. As Bush asserted, "[S]table and free nations do not breed the ideologies of murder."

Risks of Change

Nevertheless, promoting democratization in lands without a tradition of democracy carries certain risks. Democratization assistance is not a silver bullet that could solve the region's problems if we simply tried harder.

First, many of the positive attributes outlined above relate to democratic political systems once they have been established. The actual process of democratization itself is not necessarily easy and can exacerbate conflict and tensions within societies. Democratization changes the prevailing power structure, threatening the political status and gains of established elites, who then seek to protect their position and access to power. In doing so, they may appeal to religious or ethnic differences to mobilize support or to create a climate of disorder and violence that discourages any further change in favor of maintaining the status quo.

Moreover, because elections produce clear winners and losers, they can become political flash points. In cases where most economic and social opportunities lie with the state, elections can lead to violence and fraud as competitors resort to desperate measures to win power and control over resources. A process that seeks to shift the balance of power regularly in the absence of the democratic ideals of participation and inclusion is clearly vulnerable to violence and disorder—a fact that policymakers must bear in mind.

Second, in regions such as the Middle East, fair elections not only risk conflict but also the chance that election winners may be antidemocratic and anti-American. For years, U.S. policymakers have been constrained by the fear that, if Middle Eastern populations are given the chance to choose their leaders, the outcome may be worse than the status quo. The organizational superiority and ideological appeal of Islamic extremism was demonstrated in the Algerian elections in the early 1990s, when the Islamic Salvation Front was poised to gain control of the government, and more recently in Bahrain, where the last elections produced significant gains for Islamists. The commitment of these groups to encouraging further democratization is questionable at best, given their platforms and political rhetoric. (The performance of Turkey's new Islamist government, however, may prove that fears that a victory for Islamist parties will automatically lead to "one man, one vote, one time" are exaggerated.)

Zakaria makes exactly this case in his latest book, arguing that the third wave of democratization has produced "illiberal democracies" in which elected leaders have demonstrated a lack of respect for individual freedoms and rule of law. Zakaria would argue that the United States should not support democracy—by which he means elections—in the Middle East but should instead gradually encourage reform of authoritarian regimes by working to put in place the fundamentals of constitutional liberalism, rather than try to establish systems which make the state electorally accountable to its own people.

Zakaria presents an interesting historical analysis and makes a compelling and persuasive case for promoting political systems more likely to yield leaders sympathetic to U.S. interests. His argument is ultimately problematic as a guide to policymakers, however, who are grappling with how to promote a new policy toward the Middle East. First, in both academic and policy circles, the definition of democracy has long evolved beyond merely holding elections. Many of the countries he considers illiberal democracies cannot by current definition be considered democracies at all. Democratization as a process involves building a rule of law, promoting individual freedoms, and strengthening democratic institutions and culture (which Zakaria currently distinguishes as constitutional liberalism), in addition to holding free and fair elections.

Elections Are International Norm

Moreover, although elections may in fact be dangerous for short-term U.S. interests, the reality is that elections have become an internationally accepted practice. Of the 192 countries in the world, 121 are considered to be electoral democracies, meaning that they have held largely representative and fair elections. Those individuals who are struggling for reform in repressive societies in the Middle East and elsewhere genuinely desire the right to choose their own leaders. The United States, or any other outside actor, is hardly in the position to dictate to other countries that they are simply not ready for free elections.

Finally, although the United States risks undesirable outcomes in fostering free and fair elections, an alternative method has yet to be found that can predictably confer legitimacy and accountability on a government. The illegitimacy and lack of accountability of the regimes in the Middle East today breeds violent extremism and thus presents the kind of risk that the United States cannot afford to keep taking. Although the world has learned the hard way that it is counterproductive to pressure governments to hold elections prematurely—as the United States did in Bosnia—the greater value of elections cannot be dismissed completely.

Recognizing that promoting democratization, including holding elections, will not necessarily produce regimes that are sympathetic to U.S. policy interests in the short term is crucial for current U.S. policymakers so that expectations are not misguided. As regimes become more accountable to their populations, they may be less willing to back particular U.S. policies. Turkey provided the latest example when its newly elected, more representative, and more energetic parliament rejected U.S. requests for assistance in the war against Iraq.

In short, supporting democratization carries risks that must be taken into account when designing strategies for the Middle East and elsewhere. Arguably, however, there are far greater risks—particularly if one looks beyond the short term—in maintaining the status quo. The current political situation in the Middle East is primarily driven by internal realities, but it also is a reflection of past U.S. policy choices not to support democratic reforms within the region. If the United States persists in supporting friendly tyrants in the Middle East who repress their own people, the region will continue to breed extremists who argue that the United States is perpetuating the misery and frustration that characterize their everyday lives.

"Terrorism springs from sources other than form of government. There is no reason, based on the evidence of the past, to believe that a more democratic Arab world will generate fewer terrorists."

Democracy Alone Will Not Prevent Terrorism

F. Gregory Gause III

In this viewpoint F. Gregory Gause III argues that there is no empirical evidence that promoting democracy reduces terrorism. Gause argues that the presence or absence of terrorism is not affected by the form of government. According to him, terrorists will continue practicing terrorism until they achieve their goals. Gause also contends that democracy in the Arab world will result in the election of radical Islamic governments that will be hostile to the United States. Gause is an assistant professor of political science at the University of Vermont and the author of articles and books on foreign policy.

As you read, consider the following questions:
1. How widespread in America, in the author's view, is the idea that a lack of democracy is linked to terrorism?
2. What country accounted for 75 percent of terrorist incidents in free countries from 2000 through 2003?
3. In recent Arab elections, what group has emerged as the leading political force opposing the government?

F. Gregory Gause III, "Democracy, Terrorism and American Policy in the Arab World," www.ndu.edu, Institute for National Strategic Studies conference, "Prospects for Security in the Middle East," National Defense University, Fort McNair, April 20-21, 2005. Reproduced by permission.

Is there a relationship between terrorism and democracy such that the more democratic a country becomes, the less likely it is to produce terrorists and terrorist groups? In other words, is the security rationale for democracy promotion in the Arab world based on a sound premise? . . .

There is little empirical evidence linking democracy with an absence of or reduction in terrorism. [This paper] questions whether democracy would reduce the motives and opportunities of groups like al-Qa'ida, which oppose democracy on both religious and practical grounds. . . . While Arab publics are very supportive of democracy, democratic elections in Arab states are likely to produce Islamist governments which would be much less likely to cooperate with the United States than their authoritarian predecessors.

Americans Believe Democracy Reduces Terrorism

President [George W.] Bush is absolutely clear about why the promotion of democracy in the Muslim world is not only consistent with American values, but central to American interests. He laid out that logic in an address just a few months ago, [March 8, 2005] right here at the National Defense University:

> Our strategy to keep the peace in the longer term is to help change the conditions that give rise to extremism and terror, especially in the broader Middle East. Parts of that region have been caught for generations in the cycle of tyranny and despair and radicalism. When a dictatorship controls the political life of a country, responsible opposition cannot develop and dissent is driven underground and toward the extreme. And to draw attention away from their social and economic failures, dictators place blame on other countries and other races and stir the hatred that leads to violence. This status quo of despotism and anger cannot be ignored or appeased, kept in a box or bought off.

The President's analysis of the link between the lack of democracy in the Arab world and terrorism is shared across the political spectrum in the United States. 2004 Democratic presidential candidate John Kerry accepted the need for greater political reform in the Middle East as an integral part of the war on terrorism. *New York Times* columnist Thomas Friedman, America's leading commentator on foreign affairs, has done more to propound this syllogism to the attentive American public than anyone else. A senior Middle East policy maker in the Clinton Administration, after [the September 11, 2001, terrorist attacks], contended that the Administration he served had ignored the democracy issue in the pursuit of Arab-Israeli peace. . . . He said that strategy was a mistake and urged a new American policy focused on political reform. A recent book [2004] published by the Council on Foreign Relations, whose lead author was the Director of Policy Planning in the Clinton State Department, argues that the roots of al-Qa'ida are in the poverty and educational deficiencies of Saudi Arabia, Egypt and Pakistan. These deficiencies were caused by the authoritarian nature of those states, and can only be combated by their democratization. The syllogism underlying the Bush Administration's emphasis on political reform in the Middle East as a necessary part of the war on terrorism is widely accepted, and is not going to disappear when the neo-conservatives leave office.

No Evidence

While there is a logic to the syllogism linking a lack of democracy to terrorism, that logic can be challenged on both theoretical and empirical grounds. Empirically, the numbers just do not appear to bear out a close link between terrorism and the lack of democracy. Between 2000 and 2003, based on the State Department's annual *Global Patterns of Terrorism*, 269 major terrorist incidents occurred in countries classified as "free" in the Freedom House *Freedom in the World* annual report; 119 such incidents occurred in countries classified as "partly free;" and 138 occurred in countries classified as "not free." This is not to argue that free countries are more likely to produce terrorists than other countries. The free country subject to the greatest number of terrorist incidents (and, by far, the greatest number of terrorist incidents of any country in the world) is India. It is fair to assume that a number of those terrorist incidents, in Kashmir, are perpetrated by groups based in Pakistan, though clearly not all of them. It is simply to point out that there appears, at least on a first glance at the numbers, to be no clear relationship between type of government and likelihood of terrorist activity.

The case of India stands out in bold relief in these numbers. Terrorist incidents in India account for fully 75% of all terrorist incidents in free countries in the four years surveyed. A vibrant democracy with the full range of political rights available to its citizens, India has rightly been held up as an example of the possibility of democracy outside the context of wealthy Western countries. Thomas Friedman regularly asserts that it is Indian democracy which has kept extremist Islamist ideologies from dominating the Indian Muslim community. Yet, as strong as Indian democracy is, one Indian Prime Minister was assassinated (Indira Gandhi by a Sikh extremist) and a former Prime Minister campaigning to regain the office was assassinated (her son, Rajiv Gandhi, by Tamil extremists) by political opponents. If democracy reduces the prospects for terrorism, India's numbers should not be so high. It is also interesting to note that in 2003, two countries classified as "not free" accounted for 50% of the terrorist incidents in "not free" countries—Iraq and Afghanistan. At least for that year, movement toward democracy did not lessen the incentives for terrorists to operate in those countries.

Freedom Helps Terrorists

Freedom promotes or at least enables the growth of violent partisan groups, because it provides an opportunity for extremists to organize and proselytize. The point was perhaps first made by founding father James Madison over two centuries ago in *Federalist* number 10 in discussing the causes of "the violence of faction." As he put it, "Liberty is to faction what air is to fire, an aliment without which it instantly expires."

James Payne, *The American Conservative*, April 11, 2005.

More anecdotal evidence also calls into question a necessary relationship between regime type, particularly democracy, and terrorism. In the 1970's and 1980's, democratic countries generated a number of brutal terrorist organizations: the Red Brigades in Italy, the Provisional IRA in Ireland and the United Kingdom, the Japanese Red Army, the Red Army Faction (Baader-Meinhof Group) in West Germany. The transition to democracy in Spain did not eliminate ETA (Basque separatist) terrorism. Turkish democracy suffered through a decade of mounting political violence from the late 1960's through the late 1970's. In fact, a statistical study based upon data through the 1980's found a strong positive correlation between democracy and terrorism. The strong and admirable democratic system in Israel has been the subject of terrorist assault, but has also produced some number of its own terrorists, including the assassin of Prime Minister Yitzhak Rabin. Nearly every day presents a painful reminder that real democratization in Iraq has been accompanied by serious terrorism. There is a memorial in Oklahoma City testifying to the fact that our own democracy has not been free of domestic terrorism.

There is no empirical evidence for a strong link between democracy, or any other regime type, and terrorism, in either a positive or a negative direction. Terrorism springs from sources other than form of government. There is no reason, based on the evidence of the past, to believe that a more democratic Arab world will generate fewer terrorists. . . .

Terrorists Reject Democracy

There are also logical and theoretical problems, as well as these empirical problems, with the syllogism underlying the American push for democracy as part of the war on terrorism. The underlying logic of the assertion that democracy will reduce terrorism is the belief that, able to participate openly in competitive politics and have their voices heard in the public square, potential terrorists and terrorist sympathizers will not feel the need to resort to violence to achieve their goals. Even if they lose in one round, the confidence that they will be able to win in the future will inhibit the temptation to use extra-democratic means. The habits of democracy will ameliorate extremism.

Well, maybe. But it is just as logical to assume that terrorists, who rarely represent political agendas that could mobilize electoral majorities, would reject the very principles of majority rule and minority rights on which liberal democracy is based. If they cannot achieve their goals through democratic politics, why should we assume that they will privilege the democratic process over those goals? It seems more likely that, having been mobilized into politics by a burning desire to achieve a goal, a desire so strong that they were willing to take up arms and commit acts of violence against defenseless civilians in order to realize it, terrorists and potential terrorists will attack democracy and its processes if those processes do not produce their desired result. Respect for American democracy did not stop Southern slave-holders and their supporters from taking up arms in 1861. Respect for the nascent Iraqi democracy, despite a very successful election in January 2005, has not stopped Iraqi and foreign terrorists from their campaign against the new political order in that country. If the goal is important enough, it will trump democracy for some number of militants, who in turn might become terrorists.

Moreover, we know that terrorist organizations are not mass-based organizations. They are small and secretive. They are not organized or based on democratic principles. They revolve around strong leaders and a cluster of committed followers, willing to take actions from which the vast majority of people, even people who might support their political agenda, would rightly shrink. It seems unlikely that simply being outvoted would deflect them from their path.

America's major foe in the war on terrorism, al-Qa'ida, certainly would not close up shop if every Muslim country in the world were to become a democracy. [Al-Qa'ida leader] Usama bin Laden has been very clear about democracy—he does not like it. His political model is not democratic; it is the early years of the Muslim caliphate. The Taliban regime in Afghanistan was the closest in modern times to that model in bin Laden's view. In an October 2003 "message to Iraqis," bin Laden castigated those in the Arab world who are "calling for a peaceful democratic solution in dealing with apostate governments or which Jewish and crusader invaders instead of fighting in the name of God." He referred to democracy as "this deviant and misleading practice," and "the faith of the ignorant." His view of American democracy is equally negative: "The majority of you [Americans] are vulgar and without sound ethics or good manners. You elect the evil from among you, the greatest liars and the least decent . . ." Bin Laden's ally in Iraq, Abu Mus'ab al-Zarqawi, was even more direct in his reaction to the Iraqi election of January 2005: "The legislator who must be obeyed in a democracy is man, and not Allah . . . That is the very essence of heresy and polytheism and error, as it contradicts the bases of the faith and monotheism, and because it makes the weak, ignorant man Allah's partner in His most central divine prerogative—namely, ruling and legislating."

Al-Qa'ida is not fighting for democracy. Its leaders profoundly distrust democracy, and not just on ideological grounds. They know that they could not come to power through free elections. There is absolutely no reason to believe that a move to more democratic Arab states would deflect them from their course. There is no reason to believe that they would not be able to recruit followers in more democratic Arab states, as long as those more democratic Arab states continued to have good relations with the United States, made peace with Israel and generally behaved in ways that Washington hopes that they will. It is the American agenda in the Middle East, as much if not more than democracy itself, to which al-Qa'ida objects. As Washington hopes that a democratic Middle East will be a Middle East that continues to accept a major American role and cooperates with American goals, it is simply foolish to think that democracy will dry up support for al-Qa'ida.

When it works, liberal democracy is the best form of government. It affirms the dignity of each person in the right to vote. It provides the check of popular elections on those in power, along with other constitutional and legal barriers to the abuse of power. It provides for an independent judiciary to guarantee those rights and curb the abuses that inevitably come with great power. There is much to recommend it. But there is no evidence that it reduces terrorism or prevents terrorism. Regrettably, it seems that regime type has no relationship to the development or prevalence of terrorism. Thus, a fundamental assumption of the Bush Administration's push for democracy in the Arab world as part of the war on terrorism is seriously flawed.

Would democratically elected Arab governments be as cooperative with the United States as the current authoritarian incumbents? That is highly unlikely. To the extent that public opinion can be measured in these countries, we know that Arabs are very supportive of democracy. When they have a chance to vote in real elections, they generally turn out in percentages far greater than Americans do. However, we also know that the United States is distinctly unpopular in the Arab world now. If Arab governments were to more accurately reflect public opinion, they would be more anti-American. We also know that, in recent free elections in the Arab world, Islamists have done very well. Moves toward Arab democracy will, at least for the foreseeable future, most likely generate Islamist governments which will be less likely to cooperate with the United States on important American policy goals, including American basing rights in the region and peace with Israel. . . .

The trend in Arab elections is absolutely clear. In free elections, Islamists of various hues win. In elections where there is a governing party (or a royal preference, as in Jordan), Islamists run second and form the opposition. Only in Morocco, where more secular-left parties have a long history and organizational presence, was there an organized non-Islamist political bloc, independent of the government, which could compete with Islamist forces. The trends do not look like they are about to change. In the 2004 Sadat Chair-Zogby International poll, pluralities of those polled in Jordan, Saudi Arabia and the UAE thought that the clergy should play a greater role in their political systems. In Egypt 47% supported a greater clerical role, while 50% said the clergy should not dictate the political system, almost a tie. Only in Lebanon (with its large Christian minority) and Morocco did anti-clerical sentiment dominate (51% to 33% in Morocco and 50% to 28% in Lebanon). The more democratic the Arab world gets, the more likely it is that Islamists will come to power there.

It is hard to avoid the conclusion that the Bush Administration's push for democracy in the Arab world is unlikely to have much effect on anti-American terrorism emanating from that part of the world, but could help bring to power governments that will be much less cooperative with the United States on a whole range of issues (including, probably, cooperation in the war on terrorism and, most certainly, the Arab-Israeli peace process and military-strategic issues) than the current Arab regimes. Washington's democracy initiative can be defended as an effort to spread American democratic values, whatever the cost, or as a long-term gamble that the realities of governance will either moderate Islamists or lead to public disaffection from them once they are in power, as has happened in Iran. It does not serve immediate American interests either in the war on terrorism or in other important policy areas in the region.

> *"The drug of freedom is universally potent. Once the life of doublethink and self-censorship is shed, once the brainwashing stops, once freedom is tasted, no people will ever choose to live in fear again."*

Democracy Is Best for All Countries

Natan Sharansky, interviewed by Jamie Glazov

Natan Sharansky argues in the following viewpoint that freedom is for every nation, even those societies currently living under the shadow of fear. He contends that once people experience freedom, they will never again accept living in fear. If a united world stands up for democracy, he argues, freedom will prevail. Sharansky was a political prisoner in the Soviet Union. He has authored numerous books, including *The Case for Democracy: The Power of Freedom to Overcome Tyranny and Terror.* This viewpoint is based upon an interview conducted by FrontPageMagazine.com on December 17, 2004.

As you read, consider the following questions:

1. What is the author's "town-square test" for freedom?
2. What does the author mean by "doublethinkers"?
3. How does the author say political prisoners in the Soviet Union reacted to President Ronald Reagan calling the Soviet Union an "evil empire"?

Natan Sharansky and Jamie Glazov, "The Case for Democracy," www.frontpage mag.com, December 17, 2004. Copyright © 2004 by the Center for the Study of Popular Culture. Reproduced by permission.

FrontPageMagazine: What inspired you to write The Case for Democracy?

Natan Sharansky: I was inspired to write this book by those who are sceptical of the power of freedom to change the world. I felt that the arguments of these sceptics had to be answered. The three main sources of scepticism are first, that not every people desires freedom; second, that democracy in certain parts of the world would be dangerous; and third, that there is little the world's democracies can do to advance freedom outside their countries.

This scepticism is the same scepticism I heard a generation ago in the USSR when few thought that a democratic transformation behind the iron curtain was possible. Just as the sceptics were wrong then, I am convinced they are wrong now about the possibility of freedom spreading to the Middle East.

In this book, I explain why I believe in the power of freedom to transform our world. My optimism is not based primarily on the successful march of democracy in recent times but rather is based on the experience of having lived in a fear society and studied the mechanics of tyranny that sustain such a society. By helping readers understand these mechanics, I hope they will appreciate why freedom is for everyone, why it is essential for our security and why the free world plays a critically important role in advancing democracy around the globe.

You distinguish between "fear" and "free" societies. Briefly explain to our readers what you mean by this paradigm.

Freedom or Fear?

Free societies are societies in which the right of dissent is protected. In contrast, fear societies are societies in which dissent is banned. One can determine whether a society is free by applying what we call the "town-square test." Can someone within that society walk into the town square and say what they want without fear of being punished for his or her views? If so, then that society is a free society. If not, it is a fear society.

People may believe that there can be a society where dissent is not permitted, but which is nonetheless not a fear society because everyone agrees with one another and therefore no one wants to dissent. But as we show in the book, such a monolithic society, which may occasionally emerge, will not last very long. Because of human diversity—different tastes, ambitions, interests, backgrounds, experiences, etc.—differences of opinion will be inevitable. Then the society will be confronted with the fundamental question. Will dissent be permitted? The answer to that question will determine whether the society is a free society or a fear society.

Of course, there can be serious injustices within free societies. They can have all sorts of problems and abuses of rights. But by having a right to dissent and having institutions which protect that right, free societies also have mechanisms to correct those abuses. In contrast, fear societies are always unjust and have no corrective mechanisms.

Fear societies are inevitably composed of three separate groups: True believers, dissidents and doublethinkers. True believers are those who believe in the ideology of the regime. Dissidents are those who disagree with that ideology and are prepared to say so openly. Doublethinkers are those who disagree with the ideology but who are scared to openly confront the regime.

With time, the number of doublethinkers in a fear society inevitably grows so that they represent the overwhelming majority of the population. To an outside observer, the fear society will look like a sea of true believers who demonstrate loyalty to the regime, but the reality is very different. Behind the veneer of support is an army of doublethinkers.

You are critical of those who believe that democracy is suited only for certain cultures and that it is incompatible with Islam. Do you think Islam has the keys within itself to enter modernity? . . .

Does Democracy Suit All?

It is important to remember that some of the most serious thinkers once thought that democracy was not compatible with the cultures of Germany, Italy, Japan, Latin America and Russia. The great historian [Arnold] Toynbee questioned whether democracy could ever flourish out of the Anglo-Saxon world or as he put it, in "alien soil."

Let's take Japan for a moment: Truman's advisors were

very sceptical about the prospects for democracy in Japan, as were most of the "experts" of the time. And there were good reasons to be sceptical. This was a country with virtually no exposure to the West for centuries. Japan rigidly hierarchical society, and unique culture was seen as antithetical to democratic life. In fact, when the concept of rights was translated into Japan it took a compound word consisting of four characters to express it. But democracy in Japan has been a great success story. Japan is not a Western democracy. The Japanese have kept their traditions, culture and heritage, but they have joined the community of free nations.

Democracy Is the Greatest Development

Among the great variety of developments that have occurred in the twentieth century, I [do not] have any difficulty in choosing one as the preeminent development of the period: the rise of democracy. This is not to deny that other occurrences have also been important, but I would argue that in the distant future, when people look back at what happened in [the twentieth] century, they will find it difficult not to accord primacy to the emergence or democracy as the preeminently acceptable form of governance.

Amartya Sen, *Journal of Democracy*, 1999.

Still, history will only get us so far. People can always argue that the "Arabs" are different—that the sceptics may have been wrong with regard to other cultures and regions, but they will not be wrong when it comes to the Arabs and the Middle East.

And the sceptics present some weighty evidence: Twenty-two Arab countries and not a single democracy. The scenes we see on our television screens, from the celebrations that followed the [September 11, 2001] attacks to mass marches praising suicide bombers, would give even the biggest optimists pause.

But while I understand that the picture we see from the outside is very troubling, I am confident that what is really going on inside these societies is very different. Just as the 99% of Soviet citizens who supported the Soviet regime in 1985 was no indication of what the people inside the USSR really thought, the army of true believers that we think we see in the Arab world is an illusion. One only has to read the memoirs of those dissidents who have left places like Iran and Saudi Arabia to understand that these societies are steeped in doublethink.

I have no doubt that given a real choice, the vast majority of Muslims and Arabs, like everyone else will choose a free society over a fear society. Believe me, the drug of freedom is universally potent. Once the life of doublethink and self-censorship is shed, once the brainwashing stops, once freedom is tasted, no people will ever choose to live in fear again. . . .

In your book you emphasize that spreading democracy is crucial for our own security. What are some of the things that can be done to promote democracy around the world?

Moral Clarity

The two most important things that can be done to promote democracy in the world is first, to bring moral clarity back to world affairs and second, to link international policies to the advance of democracy around the globe.

When we are unwilling to draw clear moral lines between free societies and fear societies, when we are unwilling to call the former good and the latter evil, we will not be able to advance the cause of peace because peace cannot be disconnected from freedom.

By not understanding why freedom is so important to peace, we run the risk of trying to find "our dictator" in the hopes that he will provide security. In the end, we are likely to find ourselves supporting regimes that repress their own people and endanger us.

When Ronald Reagan called the USSR an evil empire he was fiercely criticized by many in the West who saw him as a dangerous warmonger. But when we in the Gulag[1] heard of Reagan's statement, we were ecstatic. We knew that once there was no moral confusion between the two types of societies, once good and evil were kept separate, the Soviet Union's days were numbered. Soon, the most fearsome totalitarian empire in human history collapsed without a shot being fired and the cause of peace and security was advanced. I

1. Soviet Russia's system of political prisons

have no doubt that moral clarity will have the same effect today and equally serve the cause of peace, stability and security around the world.

Once we have this moral clarity then we must link our foreign policies to the expansion of freedom within non-democratic societies. . . . In dealing with fear societies, the free world must have both a very big carrot and a very big stick. We should embrace leaders who embrace democratic reform and reject leaders who don't. The free world should be willing to use all its leverage—moral, political, financial, etc.—to promote freedom and democracy.

You show yourself to be quite an optimist in your book, arguing that democracy can even come to places like the Arab Middle East. Some critics argue that when we look at Arab tribal culture and its intersection with Islamism, democracy for this region appears to be an almost hopeless enterprise. Give us some encouraging words. How can we bring liberty to a region where so many individuals yearn for Sharia law and despise individual freedom, Western-style entertainment, and women's rights and equality?

I am optimistic that peace can be achieved in the region because I believe that every society on earth can be free and that if freedom comes to the Middle East, there can be peace. Thus, the potential for peace is there.

I am often asked how I can have confidence in a democratic Middle East when there are so few dissidents in the Arab world. People ask me where are the Arab [Andrei] Sakharovs and the Arab Ghandis.[2]

I would ask those sceptics to give me the names of all the famous dissidents in Stalin's Soviet Union in the 30s and 40s. Did hundreds of millions of people agree with Stalin? Of course not. There were no dissidents then in the USSR because they were all killed. Ghandi would not have had one follower, let alone millions, in Hitler's Germany. Dissent is always a function of the price of dissent. Once the price of dissent in the Soviet Union was years in prison and not death, a few hundred dissidents emerged. But they were only the tip of the iceberg. Hundreds of millions of others also wanted their freedom.

2. Sakharov was a political dissident in Soviet Russia. Ghandi led civil disobedience protests that contributed to bringing about India's independence from Britain.

The sceptics should remember that when I became a dissident in the 1970s, I knew that I could be arrested and imprisoned, but I also believed that the free world would stand with me. That is a comfort that potential dissidents in the Arab world do not have. Not only have the regimes they are confronting treated them with impunity, the free world has also remained silent.

Once that changes, once the free world encourages democratic forces within the region, once it links its policies toward states in the region to the degree of freedom they provide their own citizens, nothing will stop the march of freedom.

What will be needed is a joint effort that crosses partisan and ideological lines. In the Cold War, security hawks and human rights activists joined forces in confronting the Soviet Union. This historic partnership was critical in ending the Cold War. Today, that partnership must be reconstituted. Security hawks must understand that security and democracy are inextricably linked. Likewise, human rights activists must understand that the struggle for human rights cannot be detached from the struggle to promote democracy around the world. I believe that by bringing these two groups together, the Bush administration can succeed in its historic task of promoting democracy in the Middle East. If a united free world stands up for democracy, I have no doubt freedom, and ultimately peace, can prevail. . . .

When I was convicted [of treason in Soviet Russia in 1978], the KGB, the most powerful organization of the most powerful totalitarian empire in history, told me that the Soviet Jewry struggle was finished, that the human rights movement inside the USSR was over, that I had no choice but to cooperate. The KGB derided all those in the West who stood in solidarity with us as an army of students and housewives. But this army of students and housewives changed our world.

Less than twenty years later, the KGB is gone. The USSR is gone. Communism is gone. More than a million Soviet Jews have returned to their ancestral homeland. And hundreds of millions of people are now free. That should convince any sceptic of the awesome power of freedom, to change our world. If we believe in that power once again then the results can be no less dramatic.

"[I]f one is going to invade a country and overthrow a dictatorship in the hope of seeing democracy there in short order, one should be sure it is not a high-violence society."

Democracy Is Not Best for All Countries

James L. Payne

In this viewpoint James L. Payne argues that democracy is unlikely to succeed in cultures that experience extreme and pervasive violence. According to him, all cultures are violent before evolving into peaceful nations where democracy can flourish. In countries where this transition seems stalled, the people embrace a mind-set—characterized by intolerance and paranoia—that defeats democracy. Cultural restraint in the use of political violence is the minimum requirement for democracy to succeed, he contends. Payne has a Ph.D. in political science and is the author of *A History of Force: Why Nations Arm*.

As you read, consider the following questions:
1. What criticism does the author make about U.S. policy makers' theories on nation-building?
2. What is the difference in the provocation necessary to resort to political violence in high-violence cultures versus low-violence ones, in the author's view?
3. In terms of political violence, to what nation and century does the author compare Iraq in the early 21st century?

James L. Payne, "Democracy Is for Everyone?" *The American Conservative*, January 31, 2005. Copyright © 2005 by *The American Conservative*. Reproduced by permission.

Do we know what it takes to implant democracy in a foreign land? For over a century now, the United States has been sending troops into troubled countries and trying to establish free and stable governments. While the results have not always been disappointing, the track record overall is not good.

The results of our first effort, the 1898 intervention in Cuba, are typical. Following the Spanish-American War, the U.S. administered Cuba for four years, turning power over to an elected Cuban president in 1902. A violent revolution forced him from office, and U.S. troops came back in 1906. After more reforms and new elections, we again turned power over to the Cubans in 1909. More instability ensued, including another violent revolt. American Marines came back yet a third time in 1917, restored order, set up another constitutional regime, and withdrew in 1922. Cuba has since seen a succession of unstable and autocratic regimes, most recently the totalitarian dictatorship of Fidel Castro.

Recent nation-building efforts—in Haiti, in Afghanistan, in Iraq—seem to indicate that our understanding has not progressed since the days of the Cuban intervention. The problem isn't that we have the wrong theory about nation-building. Policymakers simply don't have any theory. The practice has been to assume that wherever U.S. troops end up as a result of this or that foreign-policy initiative, a democracy can be made to flourish. Our approach is that of hikers who set out assuming that any place they choose to stop will make a suitable campsite. Surely the time has come to question this expectation. There are bound to be countries where democracy cannot be made to succeed, at least not within any reasonable timeframe. We might save ourselves frustration, and guide policy more intelligently, if we identify those places.

While nation-builders have casually assumed that democracy can be established anywhere, scholars have gone to the opposite extreme. For them, democracy is a delicate flower that requires a host of social and institutional prerequisites from literacy, education, property ownership, and income equality to an impartial judiciary and a professional civil service. This comprehensive list greatly overshoots the mark, defining a practically perfect society not likely to exist anywhere. To understand real-world democracy, we need to put aside the wish list of academics and focus on the bare minimum needed for democracy to exist.

Restraint in Political Violence

What is that minimum? A restraint in the use of violence in domestic political affairs. In a functioning democracy, we tend to take this condition for granted. We assume that opposition leaders do not routinely try to shoot their way into power. We assume that presidents do not routinely jail and murder their opponents. In many foreign lands, however, people resort to violence in political disputes. They are willing to kill—and to risk being killed—to counter a perceived wrong or to implement what they believe to be right—or just to get themselves in power. In these high-violence societies, democracy cannot thrive.

Democracy Can Be Dangerous

People usually equate the will of the people, or the majority of the people, with good sense and basic humanity. If the average person has commonsense and is humane, the political expression of the will of the majority will be both sensible and kept within the bounds of basic moral principles. Unfortunately, people are not always kind and sensible. There are some people who are vicious, there are some who are unbalanced, and there are situations when the few who are dangerous may sway the good judgment of the many who are allegedly kind and sensible. Why this happens, and why it may be more likely to happen in one civilization than in another, is a big question, not yet conclusively explored. . . . The point we wish to make is that, because of this fluctuating situation, democracy cannot be trusted in an absolute manner.

Mordecai Roshwald, *Midstream*, February 1, 2004.

This is not to say that democracies need perfect domestic peace. They can survive instances of isolated violence. There is an enormous difference, which observers usually ignore, between an assassination carried out by a lone killer and one planned by political leaders and condoned by a large segment of the public. The former has no more political significance than a fatal automobile accident. The latter sets the stage for a civil war or a dictatorial crackdown. It is not the assassination, riot, or terrorism that identifies a high-violence society. It is the fact that these acts of violence are deliberately used as tools by some leaders in their struggle against others. Leaders who employ them are not repudi-ated; their followers excuse their bloody deeds as necessary, understandable tactics.

The idea that there are national differences in the dispo-sition to resort to political violence takes some getting used to, for it is politically incorrect to suggest that one group of people might be significantly different from another. We are not, however, speaking of a biological or genetic difference. The inclination to resort to violence is a cultural orientation transmitted from one generation to another and, as the his-torical record clearly shows, it can be unlearned.

Non-Peaceful Cultures

There's a second reason we resist the notion that some cul-tures are more politically violent than others: we assume that motives are the complete explanation for violence. At least since [philosopher] John Locke, we have been taught to in-terpret violence as the understandable response to an "intol-erable" situation. The American Revolution is a classic ex-ample. The cause of this violence is supposed to have been the justified anger of the colonists at the "long train of abuses and usurpations" of King George. Using the same logic, we say that people are revolting in this or that foreign land because they have a strong reason to: they are hungry, they are a disparaged minority, or they are fanatics who want to impose their religion or ideology.

Of course, motives, ideals, and ideologies do play a role in political violence. No one takes up the sword for no reason. But in every country, there always are possible motives for vi-olence. There are always grievances, injustices, and abuses, and there are always extreme worldviews and ideologies. What we overlook is that in some cultures, participants readily give these grievances violent form, while in more peaceful cultures the same grievances do not produce a violent reaction.

For example, a common complaint of those who start civil

wars is that they have been the victims of an unfair electoral process, that they were cheated out of their rightful victory. At first glance, this seems an adequate motive for a revolt. A closer look reveals, however, that elections in democracies frequently involve serious irregularities that the losers believe robbed them of victory. Yet they do not turn to violence. The election of George W. Bush in 2000 is an example. In addition to the claims of ballot irregularities in Florida, this election violated a core principle of democracy: the candidate [Al Gore] who obtained the most popular votes nationwide was denied victory (by the Electoral College arrangement). Many Democratic leaders were—and still are—angry about that election, but they did not turn to force to retaliate.

The point is profoundly paradoxical. In an established democracy, participants do not take up arms to protest even a transgression of democratic principles, such as a case—real or imagined—of electoral fraud. The hallmark of these societies is a relatively low disposition to resort to political violence for any reason. In a high-violence society, even apparently trivial ones, seem to provoke a violent reaction.

Who Is the Thug?

There is yet another issue that gets in the way of our ability to recognize a high-violence society: our inclination to take sides in foreign political disputes. There have been times in certain countries when one political group is a gang of thugs and almost everyone else is peaceful and decent. Unfortunately, there is a tendency to perceive all politics everywhere in these terms. We see a dictator using force to repress and persecute his opponents. Naturally we condemn him, but then, as part of the psychological mechanism of taking sides, we further assume that his opponents are blameless. Sometimes this really may be the case. But in many Third World situations, this impulse to look for "good guys" leads us to overlook the fact that many or most of the other participants are rather thuggish by democratic standards.

Iraq affords a good illustration of this process of distortion. Saddam Hussein was certainly a nasty dictator. There was no phase of violence he did not engage in, from murdering rivals and massacring minority groups to invading neighboring countries. In the process of taking sides against him, however, many observers were led to suppose that he alone was responsible for the violence in Iraq. This meant that all the other participants—Shi'ites, Kurds, and so on—were seen as blameless and peaceful. From this perspective, removing Saddam could result in a stable, peaceful regime. Unfortunately, the assumption was and is wrong. Iraq is a high-violence society. There are many participants disposed to act in thuggish ways, and their violence makes a democracy virtually untenable.

It is understandable that we should condemn the brutality of a foreign dictator. But our disapproval should not lead us to assume that the ruler is the only one in that society disposed to use force.

What Makes a High-Violence Society?

How does a high-violence society get to be that way? While a natural question to ask, it betrays a misunderstanding. It suggests that a violent politics is a variable condition, like an illness that can be contracted, gotten over, and then contracted again. As we look into the political history of different cultures, we do not see this up and down pattern. Instead, we find that all countries seem to begin as high-violence societies, and then they evolve away from this pattern. Many years ago, countries like England, France, Italy, and Norway were all characterized by an extremely violent politics. For example, the regime of Henry VIII in England was as violent and as vicious as any modern dictatorship. Henry murdered not just inconvenient wives, but scores of noblemen—even children—as well as loyal aides and advisors. Henry wasn't the only one who lived by the sword in those days. He faced revolts in Lincolnshire, Scotland, Ireland, and Yorkshire. The Yorkshire revolt was put down with the aid of a promise of amnesty, which Henry subsequently betrayed, ordering his henchmen to perform "dreadful execution" on "the inhabitants of every town, village, and hamlet that have offended." Today we call this genocide; in the old days, it was politics as usual.

Hence, a high-violence society does not get that way from any particular cause or condition. It is better understood as a country mired in the past, a country that has failed to make the transition away from a highly violent politics. When it comes to political violence, Iraq in the early 21st century is almost exactly what England was in the mid-15th century. The question we need to ask, then, is not what went wrong with Iraq, it is what went right with England—and the other areas that evolved away from the violent politics of an earlier time.

This is not a simple question. Political violence is a topic that has been all but ignored by historians and political scientists, and as a result we have very little knowledge about how and why a society evolves away from a violent politics. The best we can do at this point is to sketch out some preliminary observations.

First, the evolution away from violence appears to take a long time. It may seem from our modern perspective that political violence is wrongheaded and inefficient, and therefore it ought to be rather easy to tell people to stop it. Unfortunately, the impulse to violence is embedded in and reinforced by a broad cultural mindset, one that encompasses a host of attitudes, including intolerance, naiveté, hubris, paranoia, and emotionalism. It may not take centuries, as it did in England, to overcome this profoundly immature outlook, but it cannot be talked away in a week, a year, or even a decade.

Second, because the evolution away from violence is mainly a cultural change, it is little affected by institutional measures. The adoption of a certain kind of constitution, for example, will not make much difference. In the 19th century, countries all over Latin America copied the American Constitution on the theory that this paper document was the cause of U.S. political stability. These attempts to imitate American institutions failed to check the furious pace of revolution. England proves the converse of the point: it evolved to a peaceful politics without the benefit of any written constitution.

Change to Peaceful Culture

Third, it seems likely that growing wealth plays an underlying role in assisting the evolution away from force. As people become wealthier, they live better, and their lives are more pleasant. Hence, they begin to place a greater value on their lives and, by extension, on the lives of others. This is not, in the main, a mechanical, rational process. A man who becomes rich and comfortable does not suddenly abandon his violence-prone outlook. Instead, the effect of prosperity percolates through the culture, gradually changing the underlying perspectives related to violence.

Fourth, another factor that probably promotes the movement away from violence is communication. Communication enables observers to see the folly and waste of violence in conflicts that do not directly involve them. Again, this effect is not a direct or mechanical one. It's not enough for people to notice that a war is foolish. This perception must gradually enter thought processes and culture, weakening the attractions of war, lowering the status of professions related to war, and so on.

Fifth, the movement away from violence probably begins with the elites, since elites are the first to experience prosperity and its life-enhancing effects. Elites are also the first to benefit from communication (universities, books), and thus are likely to be the first to question the traditional emphasis on violence. The lower classes, for whom life is harder and therefore less valued, probably remain more disposed toward violence in the early stages of the society's evolution toward a peaceful politics.

A society that has made some progress toward a nonviolent politics can retrogress, for a time, when the lower classes become politically active. In 18th-century France, for example, politics within the established elites was relatively nonviolent. Political murder had been abandoned for over a century. The popular classes, however, were still strongly oriented toward violence. They carried out bloody riots and, finally, the Revolution of 1789 and endorsed and sustained the bloody leaders who came to the fore at that time.

Small Criminal Subgroups

Sixth, it is possible for a small criminal subgroup to gain control of a government in a society that has made a nearly complete transition to low-violence politics. Once in control, this subgroup may establish an extremely violent dictatorship—which gives a misleading picture of society's overall attachment to force. This is the "gang of thugs" possibility mentioned earlier.

The takeover by these violent leaders is facilitated by two circumstances: 1) a naïve, vigorous ideology that justifies extreme measures including violence, and 2) a body of lower-class followers who accept, or at least excuse, political violence. An example of this pattern was Hitler's takeover in Germany in 1933. By the 1920s, Germany had made most of the transition away from being a high-violence society. Political murder among elites was many centuries in the past, there had been freedom of the press for decades, and a number of open elections. The American reporter William L. Shirer observed, "Most Germans one met—politicians, writers, editors, artists, professors, students, businessmen, labor leaders—struck you as being democratic, liberal, even pacifist." Hitler was a deviant from this elite culture, a leader who combined demagogy and violence in a lethal brew. The pattern was similar in Italy where, again, a thug—Mussolini—used a simplistic ideology and violent lower-class followers to gain control of a basically peaceful country. Japan followed a similar route. There, a group of younger army officers, crazed by a primitive nationalistic ideology, turned to extreme violence, pushing a liberal society into a militaristic dictatorship.

In all three countries, all that was needed to have a democracy was the removal of the violent leadership cadre and discrediting of its violent ideology. The drafting of a constitution and implementing of reforms—though they may have been beneficial in themselves—were not necessary to allow a peaceful, democratic politics to re-emerge. The populace was already relatively peaceful.

These observations suggest that if one is going to invade a country and overthrow a dictatorship in the hope of seeing democracy there in short order, one should be sure it is not a high-violence society. One needs to gauge the extent to which participants outside the dictatorship group are peaceful. If democracy already was to some extent functioning prior to the dictatorship—as seen by competitive elections and relative freedom of expression—that is a sign that most participants in the country are rather peaceful and that democracy can succeed once the dictator is removed.

> "The establishment of a free Iraq at the heart of the Middle East will be a watershed event in the global democratic revolution."

Democracy Will Succeed in Iraq

George W. Bush

President George W. Bush, in a November 2003 speech before the National Endowment for Democracy, takes issue with those who argue that Middle Eastern nations such as Iraq are ill-equipped for democracy due to history or culture. Bush cites reforms occurring in the Middle East and North Africa as proof that democracy can work anywhere. He claims that democracy can succeed in Iraq, as it can in all nations, and that the democratic revolution there will send the message that freedom is every nation's future.

As you read, consider the following questions:

1. What Muslim countries does Bush cite as ones in which democratic progress has been made?
2. What specific reform proposed in Morocco does Bush cite as evidence of democratic change?
3. In Bush's view, how will democracy in the Middle East differ from Western democracy?

George W. Bush, "In Bush's Words: Iraqi Democracy Will Succeed," *The New York Times*, November 6, 2003.

Our commitment to democracy is . . . tested in the Middle East, which is my focus today and must be a focus of American policy for decades to come. In many nations in the Middle East, countries of great strategic importance, democracy has not yet taken root.

And the questions arise: Are the peoples of the Middle East somehow beyond the reach of liberty? Are millions of men and women and children condemned by history or culture to live in despotism? Are they alone never to know freedom and never even have a choice in the matter?

I, for one, do not believe it. I believe every person has the ability and the right to be free.

Cultural Condescension Is Wrong

Some skeptics of democracy assert that the traditions of Islam are inhospitable to representative government. This cultural condescension, as [former president] Ronald Reagan termed it, has a long history.

After the Japanese surrender in 1945 [after World War II], a so-called Japan expert asserted that democracy in that former empire would, quote, "never work."

Another observer declared the prospects for democracy in post-Hitler Germany were, and I quote, "most uncertain, at best." He made that claim in 1957.

Seventy-four years ago, the *Sunday London Times* declared nine-tenths of the population of India to be, quote, "illiterates, not caring a fig for politics." Yet, when Indian democracy was imperiled in the 1970s, the Indian people showed their commitment to liberty in a national referendum that saved their form of government.

Time after time, observers have questioned whether this country or that people or this group are ready for democracy, as if freedom were a prize you win from meeting our own Western standards of progress. In fact, the daily work of democracy itself is the path of progress. It teaches cooperation, the free exchange of ideas, peaceful resolution of differences.

As men and women are showing from Bangladesh to Botswana to Mongolia, it is the practice of democracy that makes a nation ready for democracy and every nation can start on this path.

It should be clear to all that Islam, the faith of one-fifth of humanity, is consistent with democratic rule. Democratic progress is found in many predominantly Muslim countries: in Turkey, Indonesia and Senegal and Albania and Niger and Sierra Leone.

Muslim men and women are good citizens of India and South Africa, the nations of Western Europe and of the United States of America. More than half of all Muslims live in freedom under democratically constituted governments.

They succeed in democratic societies, not in spite of their faith, but because of it. A religion that demands individual moral accountability and encourages the encounter of the individual with God is fully compatible with the rights and responsibilities of self-government.

Yet there's a great challenge today in the Middle East. In the words of a recent report by Arab scholars, the global wave of democracy has, and I quote, "barely reached the Arab states." They continue, "This freedom deficit undermines human development and is one of the most painful manifestations of lagging political development."

The freedom deficit they describe has terrible consequences for the people of the Middle East and for the world.

Political And Economic Failure

In many Middle Eastern countries poverty is deep and it is spreading, women lack rights and are denied schooling, whole societies remain stagnant while the world moves ahead.

These are not the failures of a culture or a religion. These are the failures of political and economic doctrines.

As the colonial era passed away, the Middle East saw the establishment of many military dictatorships. Some rulers adopted the dogmas of socialism, seized total control of political parties and the media and universities. They allied themselves with the Soviet bloc and with international terrorism.

Dictators in Iraq and Syria promised the restoration of national honor, a return to ancient glories. They've left instead a legacy of torture, oppression, misery and ruin.

Other men and groups of men have gained influence in the Middle East and beyond through an ideology of theocratic terror. Behind their language of religion is the ambition for absolute political power.

Ruling cabals like the Taliban [in Afghanistan] show their version of religious piety in public whippings of women, ruthless suppression of any difference or dissent, and support for terrorists who arm and train to murder the innocent.

The Taliban promised religious purity and national pride. Instead, by systematically destroying a proud and working society, they left behind suffering and starvation.

Many Middle Eastern governments now understand that military dictatorship and theocratic rule are a straight, smooth highway to nowhere, but some governments still cling to the old habits of central control.

Ramirez. © 2005 by Copley News Service. Reproduced by permission.

There are governments that still fear and repress independent thought and creativity and private enterprise; human qualities that make for strong and successful societies. Even when these nations have vast natural resources, they do not respect or develop their greatest resources: the talent and energy of men and women working and living in freedom.

Instead of dwelling on past wrongs and blaming others, governments in the Middle East need to confront real problems and serve the true interests of their nations.

The good and capable people of the Middle East all deserve responsible leadership. For too long many people in that region have been victims and subjects; they deserve to be active citizens.

Governments across the Middle East and North Africa are beginning to see the need for change. Morocco has a diverse new parliament. King Mohammad has urged it to extend rights to women.

Here's how His Majesty explained his reforms to parliament: "How can society achieve progress while women, who represent half the nation, see their rights violated and suffer as a result of injustice, violence and marginalization, not withstanding the dignity and justice granted to them by our glorious religion?"

The king of Morocco is correct: The future of Muslim nations would be better for all with the full participation of women.

In Bahrain last year [2002] citizens elected their own parliament for the first time in nearly three decades. Oman has extended the vote to all adult citizens.

Champions of democracy in the region understand that democracy is not perfect. It is not the path to utopia. But it's the only path to national success and dignity.

Modernization Is Not Westernization

As we watch and encourage reforms in the region, we are mindful that modernization is not the same as Westernization. Representative governments in the Middle East will reflect their own cultures. They will not, and should not, look like us. Democratic nations may be constitutional monarchies, federal republics or parliamentary systems.

And working democracies always need time to develop, as did our own. We've taken a 200-year journey toward inclusion and justice, and this makes us patient and understanding as other nations are at different stages of this journey.

There are, however, essential principles common to every successful society in every culture.

Successful societies limit the power of the state and the power of the military so that governments respond to the will of the people and not the will of the elite.

Did You Vote in Iraq's January 30 [2005] Election for the Transitional National Assembly?

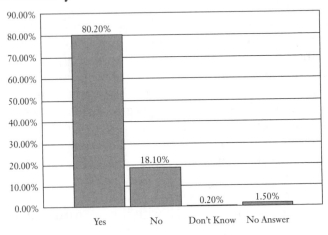

International Republican Institute survey, February 27–March 5, 2005. www.iri.org.

If You Did Vote, Do You Feel That the Election Results Reflect the Choices of the Iraqi People?

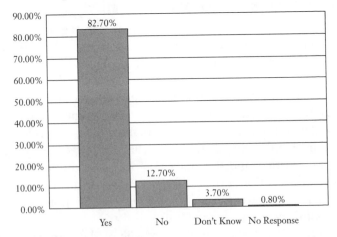

International Republican Institute survey, February 27–March 5, 2005. www.iri.org.

Successful societies protect freedom, with a consistent impartial rule of law, instead of selectively applying the law to punish political opponents.

Successful societies allow room for healthy civic institutions, for political parties and labor unions and independent newspapers and broadcast media.

Successful societies guarantee religious liberty; the right to serve and honor God without fear of persecution.

Successful societies privatize their economies and secure the rights of property. They prohibit and punish official corruption and invest in the health and education of their people. They recognize the rights of women.

And instead of directing hatred and resentment against others, successful societies appeal to the hopes of their own people.

These vital principles are being applied in the nations of Afghanistan and Iraq.

With the steady leadership of President [Hamid] Karzai, the people of Afghanistan are building a modern and peaceful government. Next month [December 2003], 500 delegates will convene a national assembly in Kabul to approve a new Afghan constitution. The proposed draft would establish a bicameral parliament, set national elections next year and recognize Afghanistan's Muslim identity while protecting the rights of all citizens.

Afghanistan faces continuing economic and security challenges. It will face those challenges as a free and stable democracy.

Building Democracy in Iraq

In Iraq, the Coalition Provisional Authority and the Iraqi Governing Council are also working together to build a democracy. And after three decades of tyranny, this work is not easy. The former dictator ruled by terror and treachery and left deeply ingrained habits of fear and distrust. Remnants of his regime, joined by foreign terrorists, continue to battle against order and against civilization.

Our coalition is responding to recent attacks with precision raids, guided by intelligence provided by the Iraqis themselves.

We're working closely with Iraqi citizens as they prepare a constitution, as they move toward free elections and take increasing responsibility for their own affairs.[1]

As in the defense of Greece in 1947, and later in the Berlin Airlift, the strength and will of free peoples are now being tested before a watching world. And we will meet this test.

Securing democracy in Iraq is the work of many hands. American and coalition forces are sacrificing for the peace of Iraq and for the security of free nations. Aid workers from many countries are facing danger to help the Iraqi people.

The National Endowment for Democracy is promoting women's rights and training Iraqi journalists and teaching the skills of political participation.

Iraqis themselves, police and border guards and local officials, are joining in the work and they are sharing in the sacrifice.

This is a massive and difficult undertaking. It is worth our effort. It is worth our sacrifice, because we know the stakes: The failure of Iraqi democracy would embolden terrorists around the world and increase dangers to the American people and extinguish the hopes of millions in the region.

Iraqi democracy will succeed, and that success will send forth the news from Damascus to Tehran that freedom can be the future of every nation.

The establishment of a free Iraq at the heart of the Middle East will be a watershed event in the global democratic revolution.

---

1. Iraq successfully held elections in 2005.

> "*For nearly 7,000 years, Iraq has been shackled to unspeakable violence, toppled pride, cruel despotic authorities, and an utter lack of self-governance.*"

Democracy Will Fail in Iraq

Edwin Black

In the following viewpoint Edwin Black argues that Iraq's long history of violence and resistance to outside interference dooms democracy in that country. Black, author of *Banking on Baghdad, Inside Iraq's 7,000-Year History of War, Profit, and Conflict,* maintains that Iraq has been plagued by uninterrupted violence and oppression since the beginning of recorded time because its natural resources have attracted the attentions of the world's colonial powers. Black claims that Iraq's violent culture and mistrust of outsiders' motives means that America's attempt to establish a democracy there will fail.

As you read, consider the following questions:

1. How does the author believe Iraq has been affected by centuries of invasion, conquest, and subjugation of its citizens?
2. What ethnic and religious groups in Iraq does the author say have been subject to mass murder or mass oppression during the twentieth century?
3. What does the author say Iraqis think is the real reason that America invaded Iraq?

Edwin Black, "Given Its History, Can We Succeed in Iraq?," www.bankingon baghdad.com, December 27, 2004, based on the award-winning book *Banking on Baghdad* by Edwin Black (Wiley 2004). Copyright © 2004 by Edwin Black. Reproduced by permission.

Amerika cannot succeed in Iraq until we understand the history we ignored and recently repeated.

Since the beginning of recorded time, Mesopotamia, that is, the V-shaped land between the Tigris and Euphrates rivers, has been a realm of uninterrupted violence and conflict. Commerce has been a leading cause. The region's schoolboy subtitle, "Cradle of Civilization," hailing back some 7,000 years, is more than misleading. Genuine civilizations clearly emerged throughout our world many millennia before Mesopotamia became the so-called "Cradle of Civilization." Archaeologists have documented civilized and highly organized cultures in ancient Jericho some 9,000 years ago, in southern France where mystic cave art was found dating back some 15,000 to 30,000 years ago, and among southern African cave dwellers some 70,000 years ago.

Nonetheless, on April 8, 1867, during a discussion at the Royal Geographical Society in London, Sir Henry Rawlinson rose to enthusiastically dub Mesopotamia the "Cradle of Civilization," largely because the region became a commanding commercial center and crossroads. This commercial attraction only raised the stakes for centuries of invasion, conquest and subjugation of its citizens.

As a result, civilization in Iraq had been stopped in its infancy. It had never matured. Instead, it became a mere cradle fit for robbery and abuse by the greatest forces in history: by the most murderous barbarians, by the most powerful nations, by the greediest corporations, by the onslaught of progress that sprang from its midst and took root elsewhere, continents away, and by the ravages of cultural self-wounding that ensured Iraq would remain a prisoner of its own heritage.

Never-Ending Violence

Indeed, for nearly 7,000 years, Iraq has been shackled to unspeakable violence, toppled pride, cruel despotic authorities, and an utter lack of self-governance. The unbreachable continuum of its legacy inculcated bitter alienation as a birthright. Rather than becoming an intersection of the most splendid and accomplished, as ancient European civilizations ultimately became, Iraq has become a crossroads of conquest and conflict.

Through it all, the people of Mesopotamia have displayed an irrepressible ability to victimize their victimizers—real or perceived—in a never-ending cycle of violence. For hundreds of years reaching into the twentieth century, even when the ruthless Ottoman Empire ruled the three ethnically diverse provinces of Mesopotamia—Mosul, Baghdad and Basra—it did so only from afar and even then only nominally. In the twentieth century alone, no group has been exempt from mass murder and/or mass oppression: Armenians, Assyrians, Baha'is, Chaldeans, Jews, Kurds, Shiites, Sunnis—all of them have felt the sting of Iraq's uncivilized impulses.

The Line of Oil

During that tempestuous twentieth century in Iraq, the region has offered only one attraction to the Western powers: oil. It has been a fatal attraction, one that has lured the Europeans, and later the Americans, deep into this troubled and tortured land.

The current saga began in WWI when Britain invaded Mesopotamia (as the three neglected Turkish provinces were collectively called) for oil and only for oil. Despite this, the British declared in their May 18, 1918 proclamation, read aloud in Baghdad: "Our armies do not come into your cities and lands as conquerors or enemies, but as liberators." Subsequent invaders would employ the phrase again and again.

As part of that wartime liberation, the British illegally seized the most valuable oil lands in Mesopotamia, the Kurdish Mosul region, this on November 7, 1918, a full week after the general armistice with Turkey. This invasion enabled Britain to cobble the three ethnically separate Ottoman provinces together—Kurdish Mosul, Sunni Baghdad and Shiite Basra—into a single land that London would rename "Iraq." The name "Iraq" came from the ancient Arab cartographic designation.

The British then established Iraq as a nation for the sole purpose of structuring the exploitation of its oil. Arnold Wilson, the British civil administrator of Mesopotamia, the man who authorized General William Marshall's unauthorized push into Mosul, wrote, "Thanks to General Marshall, we had established *de facto*, the principle that Mosul is part of 'Iraq,' to use the geographical expression . . . Whether for the woe or weal of the inhabitants, it is too soon to say." Wilson added, that had General Marshall waited just 24 hours for the restraining instructions from London to arrive, history would be otherwise. But, Wilson continued, Marshall did not wait to invade Mosul, and so "laid the foundation stone of the future State of Iraq."

Iraq Is Not Germany

Iraq's situation is not at all like Germany's in 1945 Europe. It is unlikely that any U.S. administration, let alone Bush's, has the stamina, patience and, above all, creative ideas and expertise to alone turn Iraq into a bastion of modern democracy. But now we are the middle of this maelstrom [after the 2003 war there], and a vigorous change of course in Iraq seems the only answer.

James R. Huntley, *Seattle Post-Intelligencer*, July 18, 2003.

From the Western view, Britain and France wanted to install a leader who would sign on the dotted line, thereby authorizing the oil end pipeline concessions that London and Paris had divided between them. Democracy, or a facsimile thereof, was needed to create a stabile environment for the oil to flow.

Iraqi Opposition

But Arab and Islamic nationalists in the newly invented Iraq did not want to share their land with infidel European Christians. Nor did they choose to share European values of democracy and pluralism, ideals that had never taken root in the Islamic Middle East. When Arabs hear the word "democracy," they do not think of Jefferson doctrine [named after American founder Thomas Jefferson], they hear a codeword for "we want your oil."

Indeed, the Arab world only sided with the British against the Turks in WWI as a mere expedience to obtain their national independence. Arab nationalists were willing then to speak the lingo of democratic values and trade access to cheap oil, which was worthless to them. In turn, the British were willing to blithely promise any variant of Arab national independence for that oil. But when the British liberated Mesopotamia—and then stayed on throughout the twenties as occupiers, the betrayed Iraqis exploded with terror raids, burning, bombing, kidnapping and massacring westerners, including those sent to commercially develop the land and its waterways.

Islamic militants throughout history have never hesitated to terrorize those they deemed enemies who fell within their grasp, be they Assyrians, Shiites, Armenians, Europeans or Jews.

The outraged British response to insurgent horrors was aerial bombardment to shock and awe the villages. But the Iraqi violence persisted—as did the British resolve to combat it with troops and tanks. Once again, Western involvement was tied to the thirst for the oil wealth of Iraq, and that thirst commanded. Cycles of escalation and illusory temporary ceasefires followed. But the rage and confrontation among the people of Iraq never want away.

Democracy Failed

After WWI, the British and the French, becoming ever more dependent upon oil, engineered a secret petroleum pact, sanctioned by the League of Nations, which divided up oil drilling and pipeline rights in Syria and Iraq. The oil pact was announced at San Remo the same day the League of Nations granted mandates to Britain to rule oil-rich Iraq, and France to rule Syria where the pipelines would run to the Mediterranean. The British worked hard to instill democratic values in Iraq, thus creating a stable environment for the oil to flow. But it was a governance disaster because the people did not want democracy, and resented Western efforts to impose it. Genocide against minorities, ethnic cleansing, repression, despotism, corruption and neglect was the rule in Iraq for years, perpetuating another endless cycle of victimizing and victimization.

Major John Glubb, the British officer who organized the Arab Legion, complained bitterly in a letter to Whitehall. "We . . . imagined that we had bestowed on the Iraqis all these blessings of democracy . . . Nothing could be more undemocratic than the result. A handful of politicians obtained possession of the machinery of government, and all the elections were rigged. . . . In this process they all became very rich."

They Don't Trust America's Motives

For eight more decades, the West—now with the United States joining France and Britain—has tried to hang onto its oil lifeline in the Middle East, using our best diplomats, corporate surrogates and militaries. This addictive struggle has only further fueled the cycle of insurrection and now world terrorism from a people who resent our presence and resource exploitation, and have always understood better than anyone exactly why we are there. The Arabs have come to believe that all the talk of democratic values is just a shibboleth of the infidel.

It is not sand we crave in Iraq, it is oil.

America will never succeed in Iraq, if we once again naively expect democracy to take root there and flourish. What can possibly occur in the immediate future to transform that society that has not occurred for 7,000 years?

The only way to succeed in Iraq is to survive long enough to intelligently withdraw [after the 2003 invasion], and then rapidly—at breakneck speed—develop alternative energy resources to detach us from this far-off place where we are not wanted, where we should not be, and upon which our industrialized world is now dependent.

Periodical Bibliography

The following articles have been selected to supplement the diverse views presented in this chapter.

Benjamin R. Barber "*Jihad vs. McWorld* Revisited: Opening a Democratic Front in the Fight Against Terrorism," *Berlin Journal*, Autumn 2001.

Patrick Basham "A Mistaken President," *Cato Institute*, February 4, 2004. www.cato.org.

Fares al-Braizat "Muslims and Democracy: An Empirical Critique of Fukuyama's Culturalist Approach," *International Journal of Comparative Sociology*, December 1, 2002.

Larry Diamond "Moving Up Out of Poverty: What Does Democracy Have to Do With It?" Center on Democracy, Development, and the Rule of Law, Stanford Institute for International Studies, Working Papers, Number 4, August 11, 2004.

Larry Diamond "Universal Democracy?" *Policy Review*, June 1, 2003.

Francis Fukuyama "The West Has Won: Radical Islam Can't Beat Democracy and Capitalism," *Guardian*, October 11, 2001.

Mikhail Gorbachev "Why the Poor Are Still with Us," *Global Agenda*, 2005.

Daniel T. Griswold "Does Trade Promote Democracy?" *theglobalist.com*, January 23, 2004. www.theglobalist.com.

Mathurin C. Houngnikpo "Pax Democratica: The Gospel According to St. Democracy," *Australian Journal of Politics and History*, June 1, 2003.

Rollie Lal and Sara Daly "Democracy Is the Best Weapon Against Terrorists in Pakistan," *Rand Corporation Commentary*, December 6, 2003. www.rand.org.

Chappell Lawson "How Best to Build a Democracy: Laying a Foundation for the New Iraq," *Foreign Affairs*, July, 2003.

Carol Lochhead "The Bush Doctrine: Exporting Democracy Benefits the U.S., but Using Military Might to Support Ideal Has Some Nations Wondering, What Now?" *San Francisco Chronicle*, May 4, 2003.

Greg Lowry   "The Democracy Fetish: Please Stop all the
                              Cheerleading for Democracy in Afghanistan,"
                              NationalReviewOnline, December 5, 2001.
                              www.nationalreview.com.

John O. McGinnis   "Expanding Trade: A Powerful Weapon
                              Against Terrorism," *Federalist Society for Law
                              and Public Policy Studies*, 2003. www.fed-soc.org.

Pippa Norris   "The True Clash of Civilizations," *Foreign
                              Policy*, March 1, 2003.

Colin L. Powell   "No Country Left Behind," *Foreign Policy*,
                              January/February 2005.

Brian Walden   "The Hole in Democracy's Heart: He Is the
                              Model of Villainy, but Hitler Came to Power
                              Through the Ballot Box," *Time International*,
                              April 26, 1999.

Fareed Zakaria   "How to Save the Arab World," *Newsweek*,
                              December 24, 2001.

For Further Discussion

Chapter 1

1. David Lowe maintains that democracy and freedom are spreading worldwide, but Fareed Zakaria says that democracy does not always result in more freedom. How do the two authors define democracy and freedom differently? With whose definition do you agree, and why?

2. Carl Gershman and Amy Chua disagree on whether democracy benefits developing nations. In your opinion, is it possible that democracy could benefit a nation in some ways but not in others? Explain your answer.

3. Lee Drutman and Charlie Cray argue that corporate power threatens democracy, but Daniel T. Griswold argues that corporations can foster democracy. Which argument do you find more persuasive, and why?

Chapter 2

1. Clark Moeller claims that democracy is secular while Bill O'Reilly argues that democracy is based upon religion. Explain what each author means when he refers to "democracy." How do their definitions affect your appraisal of their arguments?

2. Cathy Young argues that when politicians voice religious convictions in a campaign, they penalize secular politicians and make it seem that nonbelievers are not true Americans. Do you agree with her assessment? Why or why not?

3. Jordan Ballor says politicians should engage in religious discussions frankly because religious convictions are important to making political decisions. If her claim is true, does it follow that nonbelievers make poor political decisions? Explain your answer.

4. Amir Taheri and Fawaz A. Gerges disagree on whether Islam and democracy are compatible. Which author's views do you find more persuasive? What evidence cited by the author persuades you?

Chapter 3

1. Bradford Plumer gives reasons for abolishing the electoral college, and Tara Ross gives reasons for leaving it as it is. Identify the strongest points in each author's argument, then identify which author you find most convincing. Explain your decisions.

2. Noreena Hertz and John J. Coleman disagree on whether campaign finance laws should be reformed. How do their views on the effect campaign contributions have on elections differ?

3. Steven Carbo and his coauthors claim that felony disenfranchisement is unjust, but Edward Feser argues that it is reasonable to allow states to condition voting on following society's laws. Do you think that breaking the law should preclude an individual from voting? Why or why not?

Chapter 4

1. Jennifer L. Windsor and F. Gregory Gause III disagree on whether democracy helps prevent terrorism. In what ways do these two authors also disagree about the causes of terrorism?

2. Natan Sharansky argues that people in all countries yearn for the freedoms inherent in democracy, but James L. Payne says some countries have a history of violence that would make it difficult for them to become democracies. How could these two views be reconciled?

3. George W. Bush argues that democracy will succeed in Iraq while Edwin Black says it will not. Which author has the more compelling argument? Why?

Organizations to Contact

Acton Institute for the Study of Religion and Liberty
161 Ottawa St. NW, Ste. 301, Grand Rapids, MI 49503
(616) 454-3080 • fax: (616) 454-9454
e-mail: info@acton.org • Web site: www.acton.org

The Acton Institute is named after the English historian, John Acton (1834–1902), best known for his remark that "power tends to corrupt, and absolute power corrupts absolutely." The mission of the Acton Institute is to promote a free and virtuous society characterized by individual liberty and sustained by religious principles. To clarify the relationship between virtue and freedom, the Institute conducts seminars and publishes books, monographs, periodicals, and articles, including ones pertaining to religion and democracy.

Americans United for Separation of Church and State (AU)
518 C St. NE, Washington, DC 20002
(202) 466-3234 • fax: (202) 466-2587
e-mail: americansunited@au.org • Web site: www.au.org

The AU strives to protect separation of church and state by working on a wide range of pressing political and social issues, including religion in the schools, religious symbols on public property, church electioneering, and religion in public life. Research and resource materials on these issues can be found at the group's Web site.

Brookings Institution
1775 Massachusetts Ave. NW, Washington, DC 20036-2188
e-mail: brookinfo@brook.edu • Web site: www.brook.edu

The Brookings Institution is a private, nonprofit organization that conducts research on economics, education, foreign and domestic government policy, and the social sciences. It publishes the quarterly *Brookings Review* and many books through its publishing division, the Brookings Institution Press. Articles pertaining to democracy can be accessed on its Web site.

Cato Institute
1000 Massachusetts Ave. NW, Washington, DC 20001-5403
e-mail: cato@cato.org • Web site: www.cato.org

The Cato Institute is a libertarian public policy research foundation dedicated to limiting the role of government and protecting individual liberties. The Cato Institute is named after Cato's Letters, a series of libertarian pamphlets that Cato's founders say helped lay the philosophical foundation for the American Revolution. Cato's searchable database allows access to a number of articles on democracy.

Council on Foreign Relations
The Harold Pratt House
58 East 68th St., New York, NY 10021
(212) 434-9400 • fax: (212) 434-9800
Web site: www.cfr.org

The Council on Foreign Relations is an independent, national membership organization and a nonpartisan center for scholars dedicated to producing and disseminating ideas so that individual and corporate members, as well as policy makers, journalists, students, and interested citizens in the United States and other countries, can better understand the foreign policy choices facing the United States and other governments. It publishes the periodical *Foreign Affairs* as well as a number of books and reports. Many articles on foreign policy and democracy worldwide can be accessed using its searchable database.

electionreform.org
c/o Chris McGrath
1600 Wilson Blvd., Suite 800, Arlington VA 22209
e-mail: info@electionreform.org
Web site: www.electionreform.org

The mission of this organization is to facilitate constructive and effective changes to the American election process. It maintains a Web site designed as a source of information and a forum for discussion about the problems with the current election process in the United States. Among the issues important to this group include reform of the electoral college and campaign finance.

Freedom House
1319 Eighteenth St. NW, Washington DC 20036
(202) 296-5101 • fax: (202) 296-5078
Web site: www.freedomhouse.org

Freedom House is a nonpartisan proponent for democracy and freedom around the world. Freedom House is a leading advocate of the world's young democracies and conducts an array of domestic and overseas research, advocacy, education, and training that promote human rights, democracy, free market economics, the rule of law, independent media, and U.S. engagement in international affairs. The Web site it maintains is an excellent source of information on freedom worldwide.

Heritage Foundation

214 Massachusetts Ave. NE, Washington, DC 20002-4999
(202) 546-4400 • fax: (202) 546-8328
e-mail: info@heritage.org • Web site: www.heritage.org

The Heritage Foundation is a conservative think tank that promotes public policy based on limited government and individual freedom. The organization maintains a Web site with a searchable database that contains many articles about the issues related to democracy, including election reform, the spread of democracy, and the relationships between democracy, free trade, and foreign policy.

National Democratic Institute

2030 M St. NW, Fifth Floor, Washington, DC 20036-3306
(202) 728-5500 • fax: (202) 728-5520
e-mail: contact@ndi.org

The National Democratic Institute for International Affairs (NDI) is a nonprofit organization working to strengthen and expand democracy worldwide. Calling on a global network of volunteer experts, NDI provides practical assistance to civic and political leaders advancing democratic values, practices, and institutions. NDI works with democrats in every region of the world to build political and civic organizations, safeguard elections, and to promote citizen participation, openness, and accountability in government. It has a searchable database.

National Endowment for Democracy

1101 Fifteenth St. NW, Suite 700, Washington, DC 20005
(202) 293-9072 • fax: (202) 223-6042
e-mail: info@ned.org • Web site: www.ned.org

This group is a private, nonprofit organization created in 1983 to strengthen democratic institutions around the world through nongovernmental efforts. The endowment is governed by an independent, nonpartisan board of directors. With its annual congressional appropriation, it makes hundreds of grants each year to support pro-democracy groups in Africa, Asia, Central and Eastern Europe, Latin America, the Middle East, and the former Soviet Union. The group's Web site has numerous articles concerning the spread of democracy throughout the world.

The Pew Forum on Religion & Public Life
1615 L. St. NW, Suite 700, Washington DC 20036
(202) 419-4550 • fax: (202) 419-4559
Web site: www.pewforum.org

This organization seeks to promote a deeper understanding of issues at the intersection of religion and public affairs. It provides information on this subject to national opinion leaders, including government officials and journalists. As a nonpartisan, nonadvocacy organization, the forum does not take positions on policy debates. The Web site includes many articles on the relationship between religion and democracy, both in the United States and in Islamic countries.

The Sentencing Project
514 Tenth St. NW, Suite 1000, Washington DC 20004
(202) 628-0871 • fax: (202) 628-1091
Web site: www.sentencingproject.org

The Sentencing Project is a nonprofit organization that promotes reduced reliance on incarceration and increased use of alternatives to deal with crime. It is a nationally recognized source of criminal justice policy analysis, data, and program information. Its reports, publications, and staff are relied upon by the public, policy makers, and the media. It is especially active in opposing felony disenfranchisement.

Bibliography of Books

Dean Alger — *Megamedia: How Giant Corporations Dominate Mass Media, Distort Competition, and Endanger Democracy.* Lanham, MD: Rowman & Littlefield, 1998.

Benjamin R. Barber — *Fear's Empire: War, Terrorism, and Democracy,* New York: W.W. Norton, 2003.

David Brock — *The Republican Noise Machine: Right-Wing Media and How It Corrupts Democracy.* New York: Random House, 2004.

Stephen L. Carter — *God's Name in Vain: The Rights and Wrongs of Religion in Politics.* New York: Basic Books, 2001.

Barry M. Casper — *Lost in Washington: Finding the Way Back to Democracy in America.* Amherst: University of Massachusetts, 2000.

Amy Chua — *World on Fire: How Exporting Free Market Democracy Breeds Ethnic Hatred and Global Instability.* New York: Doubleday, 2003.

Howard Dean — *You Have the Power: How to Take Back Our Country and Restore Democracy in America.* New York: Simon & Schuster, 2004.

Larry Jay Diamond — *Squandered Victory: The American Occupation and the Bungled Effort to Bring Democracy to Iraq.* New York: Times Books, 2005.

Lee Drutman and Charlie Cray — *The People's Business: Controlling Corporations and Restoring Democracy.* San Francisco: Berrett-Koehler, 2004.

Frances Fukuyama — *The End of History and the Last Man.* London: Hamish Hamilton, 1992.

Herbert G. Gans — *Democracy and the News.* New York: Oxford University Press, 2003.

Fawaz Gerges — *America and Political Islam: Clash of Cultures or Clash of Interests?* Cambridge, MA: Cambridge University Press, 1999.

Mark J. Green — *Selling Out: How Big Corporate Money Buys Elections, Rams Through Legislation, and Betrays Our Democracy.* New York: Regan Books, 2002.

William Greider — *Who Will Tell the People? The Betrayal of American Democracy.* New York: Simon & Schuster, 1992.

Thom Hartman — *What Would Jefferson Do? A Return to Democracy.* New York: Harmony Books, 2004.

Noreena Hertz	*The Silent Takeover: Global Capitalism and the Death of Democracy.* New York: Free Press, 2001.
Samuel Huntington	*The Clash of Civilizations and the Remaking of the World Order.* New York: Simon & Schuster, 1996.
John B. Judis	*The Paradox of American Democracy: Elites, Special Interests, and the Betrayal of the Public Trust.* New York: Pantheon Books, 2000.
Marjorie Kelly	*The Divine Right of Capital, Dethroning the Corporate Aristocracy.* San Francisco: Berrett-Koehler, 2001.
Daniel Lazare	*The Velvet Coup: The Constitution, the Supreme Court, and the Decline of American Democracy.* New York: Verso, 2001.
William W. Lewis	*The Power of Productivity: Wealth, Poverty, and the Threat to Global Stability.* Chicago: University of Chicago Press, 2004.
John Lukacs	*Democracy and Populism: Fear and Hatred.* New Haven, CT: Yale University Press, 2005.
Russell Mokhiber and Robert Weissman	*On the Rampage: Corporate Power and the Destruction of Democracy.* Monroe, ME: Common Courage Press, 2005.
Dick Morris	*The New Prince: Machiavelli Updated for the Twenty-First Century.* Los Angeles: Renaissance Books, 1999.
Bill Moyers	*Moyers on America: A Journalist and His Times.* New York: New Press, 2004.
Bill O'Reilly	*Who's Looking Out for You?* New York: Broadway Books, 2003.
George Packer	*The Fight Is for Democracy: Winning the War of Ideas in America and the World.* New York: Perennial, 2003.
Greg Palast	*The Best Democracy Money Can Buy: An Investigative Reporter Exposes the Truth About Globalization, Corporate Cons and High Financial Fraudsters.* Sterling, VA: Pluto Press, 2002.
Kevin P. Phillips	*Wealth and Democracy: A Political History of the American Rich.* New York: Broadway Books, 2002.
Tara Ross	*Enlightened Democracy: The Case for the Electoral College.* World Ahead, 2004.

Steven E. Schier   *You Call This an Election? America's Peculiar Democracy.* Washington, DC: Georgetown University Press, 2003.

Natan Sharansky   *The Case for Democracy: The Power of Freedom to Overcome Tyranny and Terror.* New York: Public Affairs, 2004.

Jeffery Stout   *Democracy and Tradition.* Princeton, NJ: Princeton University Press, 2004.

Alexis de Tocqueville   *Democracy in America.* Translated by Arthur Goldhammer. New York: Literary Classics of the United States, 2004.

Joe Trippi   *The Revolution Will Not Be Televised: Democracy, the Internet, and the Overthrow of Everything.* New York: Regan Books, 2004.

Jim Wallis   *God's Politics: Why the Right Gets It Wrong and the Left Doesn't Get It,* San Francisco: Harper, 2005.

Cornel West   *Democracy Matters: Winning the Fight Against Imperialism.* New York: Penguin Press, 2004.

Fareed Zakaria   *The Future of Freedom: Illiberal Democracy at Home and Abroad.* New York: W.W. Norton, 2003.

Index